Money Magic

Money Magic

ESSENTIAL STEPS TO BALANCE YOUR BOOKS AND YOUR LIFE

PAUL LEWIS

All tax or benefits figures are for the tax year 2004/05.
They will change from April 2005.

All interest rates were correct at the time of writing on
various dates in the summer of 2004. They will change
as time passes. As will any best buys or worst buys
mentioned here.

Published by BBC Worldwide Learning, BBC Worldwide Ltd,
Woodlands, 80 Wood Lane, London W12 0TT

First published 2005. Copyright © Paul Lewis 2005

ISBN: 0 563 52201 1

Commissioning Editor: Emma Shackleton
Project Editor: Mari Roberts
Copyeditor: Miren Lopategui
Designer: Martin Hendry
Production Controller: Man Fai Lau

Set in Frutiger
Printed and bound in Great Britain by Mackays of Chatham

Contents

The love of money is the root of all evil.

1 Timothy vi, 10

Introduction

Money is one of our greatest worries. Earning it, spending it, borrowing it, saving it, but somehow never having it. Or never quite enough.

This book is about taking control of money. After all, why should bits of metal, paper and plastic, still less numbers in bank accounts, control us? Human beings invented money. And we can control it. Although it can seem difficult, it really is as simple as one two three. If you can count, you can be in charge of your money.

Money may not really be the root of all evil, but it can be the cause of anxiety, stress, unhappiness, depression and in extreme cases relationship breakdown and even death. Since it was invented in what is now Turkey around 2600 years ago it has certainly been at the heart of human activity. It may not make you happy, but it can make the bad times more bearable. And being without money can certainly make the good times a lot less enjoyable.

> Money can't buy you happiness but it does bring you a more pleasant form of misery.
>
> *Spike Milligan*

Most of us want to take control of our money. But all too often it seems to take control of us. Rent, food, fun, clothes, travel, kids, holidays, music – the list goes on. But a lot of what we spend money on we don't even know about: bank charges, interest, tax, fees, penalties. These are not things we want to spend our hard-earned on, but we do. So a few minutes (OK, a bit longer than that) spent sorting this lot out means we spend less money on these things and have more to spend on fun and family. In other words, looking after your money is win–win. You spend less on what you don't want. And more on what you do. And you don't have to work harder or earn more to do it.

This book will help you organize your money, avoid common traps, understand the way the financial world works and use this knowledge to your own advantage. Working with the grain, as Margaret Thatcher once said. It will help you see how to put your money to work. I always say that left to itself money is a lazy creature, as happy as any of us to loaf around and do no work at all. It's up to you to make your money work for its keep. There's no point in having money in the bank if it doesn't earn more. Even debt can be put to work.

So this book is the antidote to all those bleak moments when you've asked this simple question: 'Why do I never have enough money?' When you have read it and followed even some of the advice and techniques in here, you will have more. Guaranteed. And the banks will have less. Tough.

I like money. And I don't just mean I like it when I've got enough, which isn't that often. I mean I like dealing with it, thinking about it, working out how to use it – and how to stop myself, and others, misusing it. Most people don't. Which is why I've written this book. And, I hope, why you are about to read it.

The longest journey starts with a single step.

Mao Tse Tung

Chapter 1
It's your money

❑ Knowing yourself

❑ What are your financial hopes for the future?

❑ How do you pay for things you want now?

❑ Which hand do you open your purse with?

The first step is to take responsibility for managing your money. And that means knowing yourself. Let's take that first step. How much do you spend each month? Write it down now.

Now look at some of the answers below. Which is yours closest to?

- Nerds specify numbers: 'about £500' or, more frightening, 'last month I spent £623.45 and this month it will be closer to £485'. (By the way I don't use 'nerd' as an insult. Quite the opposite. Nerds, after all, brought us texting, iPods, and, in the dim and distant past, the printing press that allows you to read this book.)
- Shoppers reply: 'All that I earn' or 'Everything'.
- Jokers say: 'More than I can afford' or 'Slightly more than I earned' or just 'Too much'. Their wry smile shows they are telling the truth.
- Don't-knows shrug and tell you: 'No idea', 'Haven't a clue' or 'Not sure, to be honest'.
- Annoying people say: 'Mind your own business.' (Well, they're annoying to people who do surveys, anyway.)

These answers fall into two groups. You either know or you don't know. So Nerds and Shoppers win. The rest lose. Because knowing is the most important thing. Of course, there's more – controlling comes next. But knowing comes first.

That does not mean that Nerds and Shoppers never get into trouble with money. They almost certainly do, at least sometimes. But they win because they know what they are doing. More than 150 years ago Charles Dickens wrote:

Annual income twenty pounds, annual expenditure nineteen nineteen and six, result happiness. Annual income twenty pounds, annual expenditure twenty pounds ought and six, result misery.

Mr Micawber in David Copperfield, *1850*

In modern terms Dickens was saying: if your salary is £20,000 and you spend £20,025 you will be miserable. If you earn £20,000 and spend £19,975 you will be happy. He was right. Spending more than your income year after year is a recipe for disaster. You can put off the evil day when disaster catches up with you, but if you do not make a change, you will never be able to avoid it. So step one in any money plan is seeing what you spend and what your income is and making sure the latter is more than the former.

■ Thinking about the future

The past is a foreign country: they do things differently there.

L.P. Hartley The Go-Between *1953*

If the past is another country, the future is a different planet. Just a generation ago, who would have predicted Google? Or that the 21st century would start with 38 wars around the globe? Or that flares would be back in fashion? The future is a very, very strange place. Even stranger than the places on that exotic holiday website you look at from time to time. You know you'll go there some day. But not just yet.

One absolute certainty about the future – apart from the fact that it will get here sooner than we think – is that it will be very different from what anyone expects. And even more different from what professionals predict. But when it comes to our money, we can take some steps to control what it will be like.

Now it's time for a little exercise. No, sit down – I mean mental exercise. Write down the top three money things you want to achieve. Here's a space.

_ *properties*

_ *car*

_ *holidays*

_ *financial independance*

_ *Savings (10K – 20K)*

Over the years, people have said many things to me about their financial hopes. They normally range from fantasies to things that can be achieved by a bit of planning and work. Here is a sample. See where yours fit in.

Win the lottery Inherit a fortune Get rich	HOPING
Security Earn more, work less Retire early Not have to worry about money Have more!	ASPIRING
Buy a place to live Buy a new car	BORROWING
Pay for my wedding Have a good pension	SAVING
Something for my children Save more Have some savings Pay off my debts Pay less tax Borrow less Live within my means	PLANNING

This book can help with borrowing, saving and planning. And all those will help with the aspiring things. But the hopes? They will probably remain just that. Take the lottery, for example. In the main Lotto game, each £1 spent gives you one chance in 14 million of winning the jackpot and one chance in

54 of winning any prize. So in a typical year and a bit, buying one ticket a week means you would spend £54 and win just £10! And even if you bought 100 tickets every week, it would be nearly 2700 years before you had a 50–50 chance of winning. So don't pin your hopes on the lottery. Even in it, you are almost certainly not going to win it.

Much the same goes for inheriting a fortune. Not least because today the Chancellor takes a big chunk of estates worth more than £263,000. So unless you have very rich older relatives and they have good accountants and very few younger relatives, it probably isn't going to be you here either. As for getting rich, well, that takes skill, talent, luck and planning. At least.

Most people earn ordinary sorts of money, spend most of it, save a little of it, borrow quite a lot more, and if they are lucky manage to buy somewhere to live and have enough for a half-decent pension when they retire. It's a modest plan, but it's one we can all achieve.

I've worked myself up from nothing to a state of supreme poverty.

Groucho Marx

■ Take control

'I don't keep lists. I always lose them. They just get buried under the pile of crap on my desk.' So said a dear friend recently when we were talking about money. But lists are an essential tool in sorting out your money. It's like saying, 'I don't use a hammer. It's too heavy.' Fair enough. But you aren't going to knock in too many nails using your bare hands. Or even that old shoe you keep in the back of the wardrobe.

A list is a tool, and a jolly useful one. You can organize your money without it, but it's a lot more difficult. And clear up that crap first. It is probably hiding an unpaid bill!

A list is the first step. The second is to set goals. They don't have to be big goals – small ones will do. Spend a bit less this week. Pay off a tiny amount of debt. Try to owe a smidge less next week. Swap one bad financial product for a better one this month. Make a call, write a single letter, check your latest bank statement, overpay a tenner on your credit card. And so on.

In the 1991 film *What about Bob*?, the neurotic Bob Wiley (Bill Murray) visits a new psychiatrist Leo Marvin (Richard Dreyfuss). But Marvin is about to go on holiday. So instead of a consultation he gives Bob a copy of his new book, *Baby Steps*, which explains how to overcome neuroses by taking one tiny step at a time towards your goal. But instead of using this advice to deal with his problems, Bob uses baby steps to track down Marvin at his holiday retreat. And of course things get worse – and funnier. It's a parody. But it has a point. A baby step is one simple stage on a long and complex journey. One baby step at a time is the psychiatrist's version of the Mao quote that begins this chapter.

So don't worry if your finances look a complete mess. Or you feel weighed to the ground with debt. Or you cannot see any way of ever being able to afford even a second-floor one-bedroom flat in Leith. Or your income is never enough to meet your expenditure. There are things you can do.

And that leads on to the first Golden Rule. There are a few of them in this book.

GOLDEN RULE OF FINANCIAL ACTION

Any saving is worthwhile

Any saving is worthwhile. It might even be worth a Post-It note as well as a Golden Rule.

ANY SAVING
IS
WORHTWHILE

I know it's misspelt. But sometimes you have to draw attention even to a Post-It note. Write it down and stick it somewhere you can see it.

Now try this. Suppose you look at some page of this book about earning interest on your current account and you think it might save you a tenner. Over a year. Psshaw! as people used to say in old plays. What's the point? A tenner! It's barely the cost of a round of drinks! To which I reply: do you have a tenner on you? Take it out of your pocket or purse and hold it in two hands. Tear it into little pieces and throw it in the bin.

Well? Have you done it? If not, then you have just proved that even £10 is worth saving. Because the bad habits this book can save you from are exactly the same as throwing away a tenner. Or even a £50 note. (If you did tear up the tenner, don't worry. You can piece it back together and exchange it for a whole one at any bank. And thank you for following my advice so completely. Such readers are as gold dust.)

Look at it the other way. If you thought you had dropped £10 in the street, would you search for it, look around, retrace your steps? And when you found it would you pick it up and pocket it? And feel very pleased? You can save that £10 over and over again by following a tiny bit of this advice. Each step is just the same as searching for a £10 note you've just dropped on the street.

■ Paying for stuff
Another question. When you pay for something over £20, what do you use?

- ■ a. Cash
- ■ b. Debit card
- ■ c. Credit card
- ■ d. What's the difference?

There are three right answers to this question – a, b and c. It doesn't matter how you pay, so long as you know what you are doing. But if you put 'd', you are in big trouble. What's the difference???

Plastic cards are made of PVC, whereas cash is made of paper or metal. Har har. (And, of course, I do know that in Australia banknotes are made of a thin polymer that lasts longer and when they are worn out they are recycled as compost. But they are hard to fold and some people have proved allergic to the material used.) Seriously, however, if you do not know the difference between a debit card and a credit card, you are in trouble. Here is your cut-out-and-keep guide.

Debit card The money comes straight out of your bank account, normally the next day. It's like writing a cheque, only less trouble, and the money comes out of your account more quickly.

Credit card You borrow the money from the credit card company. At the end of the month it will send you a statement. What you pay off the debt is pretty much up to you.

So, debit cards are using your bank account and the money in it – a kind of plastic chequebook. Credit cards are borrowing money to buy stuff. An easy loan. Write the following on a Post-It note and put it in your purse or wallet, next to your cards:

DEBIT CARD = SPENDING
CREDIT CARD = BORROWING

And, you might add, using either of them is not saving!

One credit card has a new shape with one corner curved instead of square. If they were honest, all credit cards would be shaped like a shark's fin. These efficient but brainless machines prey on money. They don't care where it comes from. And they cost an arm and a leg.

■ Wanting and having

Another question. When you want something that you cannot afford out of your monthly income, do you ...?

1. Save up for it then buy it.
2. Apply for a zero per cent credit card and use that to buy it.
3. Forget about it.
4. Wait for a Christmas/birthday/anniversary and ask your beloved to buy it for you.
5. Get a loan from your bank, making sure you can afford the monthly repayments.
6. Take out the credit deal the shop offers you.

7. Use your debit card and just go overdrawn.

8. Write a cheque using your cheque-guarantee card.

9. Use your existing credit card and hope you can pay it off some time.

10. Steal the money.

How did you answer? Take the number of your answer away from 10 to find out your score. If you answered number 6 (shop credit), 10 − 6 = 4: you get 4 out of 10. Not a good score. If you answered number 10 (steal it), you get nought. Move directly to jail. Do not pass 'go'. If you answered number 1 (saving up), you score 9 and are a bit of a hero, and the only reason you don't get 10 out of 10 is to stop you becoming a bighead. Write down your score now. And then read on to see why you got that score.

Score: 9 Saving up for stuff is what people used to do. Before credit became so easy, it was the only way to buy things. For people without access to credit, it still is. If you take this course, give yourself one gold star. And make sure that the money you save is in an account where it is earning interest – preferably tax free (see Tax-free savings, page 153). If you do that and don't spend it on anything else meanwhile, and don't go overdrawn struggling to save up, then award yourself a 10.

Score: 8 A zero per cent credit card is the closest thing to free money this side of a tree that grows tenners. Nevertheless, you should only use it if you work out what it will cost you over six months (or as long as the free debt lasts) and strictly pay off that amount each month until the debt is cleared. Then cut up the card. You only score 8 because there are risks – like missing a payment, going on too long, etc. But if you success-fully avoid those traps, you can award yourself 9½. More on zero per cent offers in Free credit on page 114.

Score: 7 If you forget about it you are a saint, and very good with money. The best way to save money is to want less. It's a bit like dieting. Much easier if you don't want to eat, or, if you do, you control your urges. Just as hunger is your body's way of saying you're losing weight, so want-ing stuff and not buying it is nature's way of saying you're controlling your money. So why only 7? Because you probably can't do it for ever.

Score: 6 Asking for it as a present is a good approach if you have a kind loved one who is able to afford it. But it won't always work, and, of course, you don't want your loved one to go into debt for you, do you? Well, do you? And there will come a moment when they want – or perhaps feel they should be given – a similar present. So in a way it puts the problem off rather than solving it. Or converts a financial problem to a relationship problem. (More on that later.)

Score: 5 A bank loan can be a good deal. The big advantage is that the repayments are certain – you can budget for them. Make sure that the interest rate you pay is good and never take out the payment insurance, which can double the cost of the loan. And remember the Golden Rule of Borrowing – see opposite, and page 110. You only get half marks, though, because there are better ways to borrow.

Score: 4 Shop-bought credit is almost certainly a bad idea for three reasons. The salesperson will be on commission and as likely as not will earn more from selling you the credit than they do from flogging you the goods. It is really difficult to refuse it. In addition you will usually be pressured to take out insurance on the loan payments (more commission), and on the goods you have just bought (still more commission). Avoid this triple whammy. Much better to go into the shop knowing how you are going to pay. And when you are offered extras, take Nancy Reagan's advice and just say no. Don't be like Monica Lewinsky, who said, 'Sure!'

Score: 3 Debit cards are ways of paying not borrowing. Where's that Post-It note? But you can use a debit card and end up borrowing as well as paying. When the shop swipes your card and you sign or put in your PIN, the card is checked with your bank to make sure it is valid and you have enough money in your account to pay for what you have bought. Well, sort of. You might think it would be sensible for every transaction to be checked to make sure you have enough money to pay for what you have bought. But that doesn't happen. If your purchase is below a certain amount, the shop does not check with your bank at all. It's called a floor limit, and every shop chooses its own. In some big stores, amounts under £100 may not be checked online. You can even get cashback without a check sometimes. And even if the shop does check, your bank might decide to authorize the payment even though it does take you a bit overdrawn. And there's a third problem. The check is done on the day of purchase. But the debit from your account normally happens the next day. Meanwhile, standing orders and direct debits may have come out of your account, leaving you overdrawn. And perhaps paying a £25 penalty. So just paying by debit card and hoping you can sort out the overdraft later is not a good idea. Debit cards are for paying, not for borrowing. Write it on the back of your hand now.

Score: 2 Using a cheque has some advantages. But using a cheque with a guarantee service knowing the cheque will bounce is not good. It is just as bad as using a debit card. And don't tell me, please, that the cheque won't clear for three days. I know that. But nor will the payment you are sure will be going in tomorrow. If it's that close, wait until tomorrow. You don't really deserve even 2 out of 10.

Score: 1 So you use your existing credit card and hope you can pay it off. Hmmm. There is a Golden Rule of Borrowing. Never borrow to buy something over a longer period than the item will last. More on this golden rule, and debt and borrowing, in Chapter 6. But for now, I'll just say this: buying thoughtlessly on your credit card is very bad. 1 out of 10. Don't do it.

Score: 0 Of course you wouldn't steal to pay for anything, would you? Who do I think you are? Actually, writing a dud cheque or using a debit card with nothing in your account is stealing. Just not so obvious. It is, after all, taking money without permission. That's why I put this in. So I could give a bit of a lecture. Consider it done. Won't happen again. Probably.

■ Money and the two brains

Now we're going to do something a bit different. Which hand do you open your purse with? Pretend you are about to pay for something. Get out your money or your card. Do you use your left hand or your right? And when you hand over the card or cash, do you then use the other hand? Purse in your left, money in your right. Wallet in your right, card in your left. Write down which it is.

The reason for doing this becomes clear a bit later. But first, some psychology. Most people know there are two halves to the brain. And that one side – the left – is supposed to be more logical, while the other, right-hand side, is more creative. Other words associated with the two halves are these:

LEFT BRAIN	RIGHT BRAIN
Logical	Intuitive
Reality	Fantasy
Talking	Daydreaming
Doing sums	Drawing
Solving puzzles	Imagining a beautiful sunset
Reading	Listening to music
Objective	Subjective
Verbal	Visual
Use words to remember things	Remember things by using pictures
Highly organized	Lacking organization
Plan ahead	Impulsive
Good spelling	Bad spelling

LEFT BRAIN	RIGHT BRAIN
Read the manual	Try stuff out
Keep track of time	No sense of time

Notice that the words for the left brain are all lined up neatly on the left, and the words for the right brain are all centred. That's very left-brain/right-brain too.

The two halves of the brain are not equally balanced. In some people the left brain dominates, while other people find it is the right-hand half that is more important. You may have heard artistic people called 'right-brained', and scientists called 'left-brained' or sometimes just 'brainy', because we do tend to value left-brain skills more. There are two things that left- and right-brain people have in common, however: when they read this list they can both place themselves as either left- or right-brainers. And they both think their way of doing things is the best.

■ Are you a leftie or a rightie?

No one knows whether we are each born with a dominant left or right brain or whether we simply get into the habit of preferring one half of the brain to do what we grandly call 'thinking' – which is really just processing information. Some tasks are associated with one half of the brain and some with the other, and a good way to find out if you are a leftie or a rightie is to see which you prefer. And the best way to do that is to use a forced-choice test. In other words, you are not allowed to say feebly, 'Well, actually, I like doing them both.' No, we want decisiveness here (this is a bit of a left-brain book), and so you have to make a choice. And write down the answer.

1. Do you prefer attending a lecture or going to a concert?
2. Would you rather draw a flower or solve a puzzle?

3. When you buy equipment, do you read the manual or try it out?

4. On a holiday morning do you plan the day out or see what it will bring?

5. If you meet someone new, are you better at remembering their face or their name?

6. When you go to the supermarket, do you remember what you need or take a list?

7. Would you rather watch a ballet or write your diary?

8. Which do you do first, easy stuff or the important things?

9. In a strange area, do you go by your sense of direction or carefully follow the map?

10. On a new website, do lots of graphics annoy you or please you?

OK. Now look at the table below. Then write down 1 each time you gave the left-brain answer and 0 each time you gave the right-brain answer.

LEFT BRAIN	RIGHT BRAIN
1 Attend a lecture	Go to a concert
2 Solve a puzzle	Draw a flower
3 Read the manual	Try it out
4 Plan the day	See what the day brings
5 Remember their name	Remember their face
6 Take a list	Remember what you need
7 Write your diary	Watch a ballet

LEFT BRAIN	RIGHT BRAIN
8 Important things first	Easy things first
9 Use a map	Use your sense of direction
10 Lots of graphics annoy	Graphics are fun

Add them up. What's your score?

0–2 strong right brain
3–4 moderate right brain
5 balanced brain
6–7 moderate left brain
8–10 strong left brain

■ And my point is?

So what has all this got to do with money? Two things. Each very different.

Left-brain people are much more likely to make lists, write things down, buy what they can afford and be organized. Right-brain people are more inclined to buy what they want, worry about it later, keep things in their head and act intuitively. So the theory goes. And this may mean that right-brainers need to work that little bit harder to control their money.

But there is another way of looking at the way each side of your brain controls the way you handle money. Each half of the brain controls the opposite side of the body. The left-hand side of your brain controls the right-hand side of your body, and the right-hand half controls your left-hand side. Even your eyes are divided in two, though here it gets a bit more complicated. Each eye is divided so that the left side of the brain processes things you see in the right-hand half of the world. And the right brain sees the left-hand half of the world. It is an odd way of arranging things, and it's unique to higher mammals, including apes and, of course, humans.

Most of the time we don't notice any of this thanks to a massive bundle of nerves that links the two halves of the brain and passes data from one half to the other. It's called the corpus callosum. (And if you find that interesting you are probably a left-brain person.) In case you are wondering, left-handed people have a much bigger corpus callosum – the extra connections seem to make them more versatile. So if you are left-handed, ignore those horrid people who call you sinister, gauche or cack-handed – or *mancino* (Italian) or *zurdo* (Spanish) or *vasenkatinen* (Finnish), etc. They're only jealous.

But left- or right-handed, what you do with your right hand and see on the right side is controlled by the left, logical side of your brain. And what you do and see on the left side of the world is more controlled by the right, more creative half of your brain. If you look back at the table on page 22, that should make your right hand objective, organized and logical, while your left hand is more subjective, intuitive and impulsive.

So now you see the point. Which hand do you use to pay with?

Try it. Are you a right-hand payer, using your logical left brain? Or do you pay with your left hand, guided by your intuitive right brain?

Now, I'll be honest with you. I am not at all sure how significant that is. An American scientist called Roger Wolcott Sperry was given a Nobel Prize in 1981 for his work on the differences between the two halves of the brain. So the left-brain/right-brain stuff is well grounded. But how that translates into which hand we use to do things is much less clear.

For example, I keep coins in my left-hand trouser pocket and notes in my right. I've done it for years. I like cash. When I pay with notes, I get them out with my logical right hand. But I hand them over with my intuitive left hand. And when I get coins out, I put them in the palm of my right hand and still hand them over with my left. I also like paying with the plastic cards I keep in my wallet, which could be anywhere – in a pocket or my bag. But I always hold my wallet with my intuitive left hand and pay with my logical right hand. That should mean that I spend intuitively with cash and logically with plastic. Maybe I do take more care with the big things. Which is just as well, as the more expensive things are generally bought with plastic. Maybe I'm well balanced. Or maybe it's all nonsense. But think about which hand you use, and ask your friends what they do. And see who is best with money.

The next chapter has a practical use for all this. But the main conclusion of this chapter is:

One step at a time. One goal at a time.

Be patient. We are heading for the long road towards managing our money. Next, what we spend.

Money talks.
Even if it is just
to say goodbye.

Anon

Chapter 2
Where it goes

❏ Know what you spend and why

❏ How to avoid habitual spending

❏ Using cash to manage your money

Taking control of your money is simple. Don't get me wrong. I'm not saying it's easy. It isn't. If it was, we would all do it. But it is simple. People often confuse these two words but they are very different.

Simple = straightforward
Easy = without difficulty

This book explains the simple bit – how to do it. And leaves to you the difficult part – doing it.

It's a bit like losing weight. All that material we call our body has been made out of what we eat and drink. So if we want less body we have to put less down our throats. It's that simple. And, of course, that difficult.

How often have you run out of cash and said to yourself: 'I don't know where it's gone. I only went to the cash machine yesterday.' Then you rack your brains to try to work out where it went. You even try to write it down. But the arithmetic never adds up, does it? You can never manage to write down all the things you bought and make it come to the £30 you know you took out just 24 hours ago. And it's not as if you've *been* anywhere!

■ Knowing what you spend

Step one of controlling your money is knowing what you spend. And for most of us the only way to do that is to write it down. Not at the end of the day, but as we spend it. Yes, I'm talking about a spending diary. Here's how it might go for a typical day at work for someone who travels to work in their local town or city.

OLD YOU SPENDING DIARY

Time	Place	What	Price
7.30am	Leave home		

Time	Place	What	Price
7.40am	Station/bus stop	Newspaper Sweets	£0.60 £0.45
8.30am	Starbucks	Cappuccino Croissant	£2.70 £1.15
11.00am	Work (bored)	Tea (subsidized) Biscuits for colleagues	£0.30 £0.70
1.00pm	Pub	Lunch	£8.25
2.00pm	Starbucks	Espresso	£1.25
3.00pm	Work (tired)	Tea (subsidized) Bottled water Chocolate	£0.30 £0.75 £0.65
4.15pm	Work	Leaving present	£5.00
6.00pm	Pub	Quick drink with Sally Crisps	£5.00 £0.65
7.30pm	Station/bus stop	Evening paper	£0.40
8.15pm	Corner shop	Milk, bread, ice cream	£2.54
8.20pm	Back home		
Total			**£30.69**

Oh, so *that's* where it went! £30. And look at that list carefully. Not a single thing there will last until tomorrow. If you did that every working day for a year you would spend £6900. And to have that much left after taxes you would need to earn £10,300. So cutting out all that spending would be like getting a pay rise of ten grand. And remember, this money is *before* your rent or mortgage and your travel-to-work costs are taken into account. And you haven't even been shopping yet! Working can be expensive.

So how do you cut down? The things on the list are nice. You work hard, you deserve them. Maybe. But can you afford them? Here is the list again with the annual cost of each item – assuming you work 225 days a year, which allows for four weeks' holiday, eight public holidays and seven days off sick. The right-hand column shows the amount you have to earn to pay that out. Remember, a third of everything you earn goes in tax before you see it – 22 per cent on income tax and 11 per cent on National Insurance. So for every £100 you spend on something, you need to have earned nearly £150. Out of your earned income of £150, £33 goes on tax and £16.50 on National Insurance, so you get £100.50 to spend. The Chancellor of the Exchequer gets the rest.

OLD YOU SPENDING DIARY

What	Price	Cost per year	Equivalent in pre-tax earnings
Newspaper	£0.60	£135.00	£201.49
Sweets	£0.45	£101.25	£151.12
Cappuccino	£2.70	£607.50	£906.72
Croissant	£1.15	£258.75	£386.19
Tea (subsidized)	£0.30	£67.50	£100.75

What	Price	Cost per year	Equivalent in pre-tax earnings
Biscuits for colleagues	£0.70	£157.50	£235.07
Lunch	£8.25	£1856.25	£2770.52
Espresso	£1.25	£281.25	£419.78
Tea (subsidized)	£0.30	£67.50	£100.75
Bottled water	£0.75	£168.75	£251.87
Chocolate	£0.65	£146.25	£218.28
Leaving present	£5.00	£1125.00	£1679.10
Quick drink with Sally	£5.00	£1125.00	£1679.10
Crisps	£0.65	£146.25	£218.28
Evening paper	£0.40	£90.00	£134.33
Milk, bread, ice cream	£2.54	£571.50	£852.99
Total	**£30.69**	**£6905.25**	**£10,306.34**

Let's look at all the things as they appear in the table, one by one.

Newspaper You listened to the radio while you got up – you know what's going on. And aren't there papers in the common area at work? Don't buy it. It costs you £135 a year! Take a book to read. And if you want a new one, get it from the library.

Sweets Need I say anything?

Cappuccino It is nice: the caffeine perks you up, and the milk is nourishing. But is it worth £2.70? Take a flask. Just saving £2.70 a day is like a pay rise of £900 a year. And the croissant? Suppose your boss said she'd give you a £386 pay rise as long as you didn't eat a croissant on the way to work for a year? Say no to the pastry. You'll be happier.

Tea Good value, it's subsidized. Buy it when the flask runs out.

Biscuits for your friends A kind thought, but are they worth £157 a year? Take turns. Do it occasionally.

Lunch Sociable lunches are nice, but home-made sandwiches are cheaper. And you can all sit together and eat them. Once you start bringing them, others will follow suit. And if you must have a 'meal', then try the subsidized staff canteen, if there is one. And no espresso afterwards.

Bottled water Another waste of money. All workplaces have drinking water and many now provide their own water fountain. OK, so you prefer it fizzy. But is the fizz really worth buying a bottle a day – the equivalent of spending a pay rise of £250 a year? For water!

Chocolate needs no comment at all.

Leaving present A fiver was kind, especially as you didn't actually know Pete that well (and didn't like him, but you should probably ignore that). Of course, this doesn't happen every day – though it does seem that almost every week someone is pregnant, engaged, a year older or leaving. And don't be ashamed of giving £2. Clink, don't rustle, when someone leaves.

Sally is a nice girl, you get on, and a midweek drink does help things along. But not every day. And just have one drink, not one each – her turn next time. And no crisps.

An evening paper really isn't needed. You have a radio and a TV, plus you can spend your journey writing your money diary – though that will occupy less time as you spend less.

Milk, bread and ice cream All three are best bought in a weekly shop at a supermarket and put in the freezer. A full fridge is cheaper to run than an empty one. OK, so you don't buy these items every day. But there is always something you need, isn't there? Cutting corner-shopping saves money.

So a year from now your spending diary might look like this.

NEW YOU SPENDING DIARY

Time	Place	What	Price	Cost per year	Equivalent in pre-tax earnings
7.30am	Leave home				
7.40am	Station/ bus stop	No newspaper	£0.00	£0.00	£0.00
		No sweets	£0.00	£0.00	£0.00
8.30am	Avoid Starbucks	No cappuccino	£0.00	£0.00	£0.00
		No croissant	£0.00	£0.00	£0.00
11.00am	Work (bored)	Tea (subsidized)	£0.30	£67.50	£100.75
		Biscuits for you	£0.25	£56.25	£83.96
1.00pm	Avoid pub lunch	Sandwich (home-made)	£0.50	£112.50	£167.91
2.00pm	Avoid Starbucks	No espresso	£0.00	£0.00	£0.00

Time	Place	What	Price	Cost per year	Equivalent in pre-tax earnings
3.00am	Work	Tea (subsidized)	£0.30	£67.50	£100.75
		No bottled water	£0.00	£0.00	£0.00
		No chocolate	£0.00	£0.00	£0.00
4.15pm	Work	Leaving present[1]	£2.00	£450.00	£671.64
6.00pm	Pub	Quick drink with Sally	£2.50	£562.50	£839.55
		No crisps	£0.00	£0.00	£0.00
7.30pm	Station/ bus stop	No evening paper	£0.00	£0.00	£0.00
8.15pm	No corner shop	Milk, bread, ice cream from supermarket[2]	£1.75	£393.75	£587.69
8.20pm	Back home				
Total			£7.60	£1710.00	£2552.24
Saving			£23.09	£5195.25	£7754.10

[1] OK, not every day, but there's always something, isn't there?
[2] And you shouldn't be eating ice cream every day anyway!

This shows a saving of £23 a day, which is nearly £5200 a year. And remember, that is the same as having a pay rise of just over £7750.

Now, you may be feeling a bit smug. None of this is really you. You live close to work. You do not pass Starbucks; you don't like newspapers or croissants or chocolate. And you simply don't believe you spend £30 on nothing in a working day. Good. But don't feel smug yet. Try the working-day diary and see what you *do* spend. Then multiply it by 225 to get the annual cost. Then multiply it again by 1.5 to get the amount you have to earn before tax in order to spend that much, and you'll feel a bit differently. And, of course, the working day is only the start.

■ Other spending

Naturally, your spending diary has to cover more than this. What we spend at work is just the start. So it is important to write other things down too. Cash expenditure is the most important thing to note down carefully. Things you pay for with a debit or credit card or with a cheque are less important to note because you will get a statement listing them – though we've all had that experience of checking statements and wondering what on earth that entry 'ABCD £49.99' was for. So write them in your diary, and keep your receipts. Pretty soon you will realize what kind of things take your money.

> Too many people spend money they haven't earned to buy things they don't want to impress people they don't like.
>
> *Will Smith*

Shopping I don't mean food – though we will come to that in a minute. I mean shopping. We all have a weakness. With many of us it's clothes or CDs. Others like books or sports stuff. Some must have the latest computer games. Maybe you have a car or a motorbike you just have to buy things for. Or a pet. And then there are those little things for your home: cushions, bedding, flowers. I'm not going to tell you to spend less on any of these or to rush around like a honeybee trying to find the lowest price, though it can be done and it can save money. But all I ask is that you add up what you spend. Remember this is regular spending. Stuff you buy every month or more, in the course of normal recreational shopping.

Children This is the big divide. People with children have a lot more spending to do than those without. Everything you want, they want – in spades. Tiny clothes seem no cheaper than adult-sized ones, small mouths seem to eat as much as big ones, and the appetite for toys, games and trips out is never-ending.

Recreation The pub, meals out, seeing friends, parties, football, sport, cinema, theatre.

Home supplies Just about anything you buy at the supermarket: food, drink, washing powder, toiletries. All those essentials.

Travel Buses, trains, trams, the tube; and, of course, cars and bikes need petrol. (Stop looking smug, you cyclists! Even that old bike needs maintaining and you need a helmet from time to time.)

> **Just writing everything down and adding it up**
> **will act as a brake on spending. In some ways, it is**
> **like a diet. If you write a food diary, you eat less.**
> **If you write a money diary, you spend less.**

All this so far is what I call day-to-day or at least month-to-month spending. You buy it regularly so it has to come out of your monthly money. And these are things you actually pay for – you hand over the cash or the card. Then there are all those payments that just seem to leave your bank account without your knowing anything about it. In goes your money each month or week, but it's like putting water in a colander. To list these items you need to look at your bank statement and your credit-card statement. I hope you have them in a file somewhere. If not, and you hate filing, why not consider moving all your banking online? See Online banking, page 48, for how to do that and why it's a good idea.

Bank If you have a credit card, a bank account or a loan, there will be money going out to the bank each month. Write it down. But sit down first. It may be a lot more than you expect. Some of it will be interest, some will be charges, some will just be there. If there's anything you don't understand, ask the bank. Sometimes penalties are added wrongly and a quick call will get them taken off.

Household bills Most of these expenses come out of your bank account through direct debit. Rent, mortgage, council tax, gas, electricity, water – work out the amount each month. And if they don't come out through direct debit, why not? You normally get a discount if you pay that way.

Communication What? Well, your fixed-line phone, your mobile phone, Sky or cable TV, internet access. One survey found that we spend as much on our mobile phone as we do on gas and electricity. Again, these charges normally come out on direct debits.

Direct debits are very convenient ways to pay – especially for the companies taking the money out of your account. That is why they may offer a discount if you pay that way. I am not against direct debits. They are very convenient for us too. But direct debits are like fitting a little back door to your bank account that someone else has the key to. And that means you lose some control over your own money. We saw that earlier with debit cards. You can pay for something today when you have the money. But by tomorrow the electricity supplier or the mobile phone network has helped themselves to a monthly payment and you are overdrawn. So you need to make sure you have an up-to-date list of all the regular payments that are taken out automatically so that you know where you stand throughout the month.

The other thing people worry about with direct debits is that the company will take too much. If that does happen, and it is very rare, banks guarantee that they will refund the money. So even if the company that takes it is fraudulent or goes bust, you should not lose anything.

Then we come to the big things. Washing machine. Fridge. Audio equipment. Cameras. Computers. A car. Holidays. And don't forget Christmas and big family birthdays and anniversaries. I expect you feel tired just looking at the list of stuff we all buy – that we all think we need. Now, however, there is a bit of arithmetic to do. Have you got all your sums together?

Now look at these different types of expenditure and multiply (or divide) your sums as indicated.

Daily stuff (work etc) x 225
Weekly stuff (weekend treats, Friday night out) x 50
Monthly stuff (big clothes shop, DVD, direct debits) x 12
Quarterly stuff (bills you pay quarterly) x 4
Annual stuff (holiday, Christmas, every birthday, water bill) x 1
Every few years (washing machine, fridge, vacuum cleaner, audio, camera) ÷ 5.

Add them all up. Then divide the total by 12. Then pick yourself up. That's what you spend each month. Is it more than your income?

Yes? Then you have two choices. Cut your spending, or increase your income. Or – I know I said there were two choices but wait for it – or go into debt and read Chapter 6 NOW!

If you hated all that times 225 divide by 5 stuff, don't worry. Everyone who has ever been to school or been a teacher or had children knows that arithmetic is not the most popular subject for most people, though strangely there are those who love it. Doing your accounts does involve arithmetic, but it's nothing difficult. We're not talking maths here. Just some basic adding up. As in 2 plus 2. We all know that. It's 4. And taking away, like 2 minus 2. Which is nought. Or nothing.

Of course, in finances you can have less than nothing. You can owe someone money, usually the bank. If you have £100 in your bank account and you spend £100, you have nothing. If you spend £200 you have minus £100 – in other words, you owe the bank £100. Owing the bank – having minus numbers in your account – is what this book will help you stop. So adding and subtracting are the main things you need to do to control your money, though multiplying and dividing are handy, too. But all you need is a calculator. If you don't have one, then buy one. Calculators are cheap, last for years and do all the arithmetic for you.

■ Cash flow

Cash is a poor man's credit card.   *Marshall McLuhan*

Some of the best managers of money in the world have very little of it. People who live on very low wages or on income support have to be good managers, have to control spending and have to know when the money runs out. And they do it in a very simple way: with cash. It's a long time since wages were paid in cash and even social security benefits are now normally paid into a bank account. But in the past cash was king. You got paid on Friday in notes and coins. And if it ran out before the next Friday, then you just didn't have any money to spend.

Today money means figures on a bank statement, numbers on a computer somewhere. Notes and coins are a way of spending it, but not normally a way of controlling it. It's the digital age. But you can turn back the clock. And use those bits of paper and metal to control your spending. So rather than visiting the cash machine – even the name implies it makes the money! – whenever you are a bit short, try taking out a certain amount for the week.

The average amount taken out of a cash machine is £60. But a quick survey of a group of friends told me that they take out much less – £30 or even £20. That may not mean they spend less. They just visit the machine more often. One friend is the exception. He hates plastic cards. He gets cash personally from the bank with a cheque, and always asks for £50 notes. He uses that for all his spending. He thinks he's careful. I think he's a bit mad.

But why not try working out how much you want to spend in a month? Then divide it by four and take that much out each week on a Monday. And swear to yourself you will not visit that machine again – or use plastic – until the following Monday. It's important that you take the cash out on a Monday. If you do it on a Friday you will spend it all at the weekend. But if you do it on a Monday it will motivate you to keep some back for weekend treats.

You remember that left-brain/right-brain stuff? Whatever you answered to those questions, try this experiment. Keep your cash and your cards somewhere new. Put your purse in a different part of your bag. Move the cards and cash around in your purse. Keep your wallet in a different pocket. The cash you carry around – put it somewhere else. If you keep it in a purse, put it in a pocket. And vice versa. Whichever hand you normally pay with, use the other one.

When you try this, you'll discover that we have very strong habits about where we put our money, which hand we use to reach for it and which hand we use to pay with. So if you change where you keep your cash and cards and how you pay, it will feel very strange. And that will give you a little pause before you part with your money. And in that pause you can think, Is this spending sensible? Do I need that 38th T-shirt? Is that £49.99 bit of software for the computer really necessary? Will I listen more than once to that £14.99 CD? It is not abstinence or self-denial we are talking here. But it is pause for thought. Whether you believe the left-brain/right-brain stuff or not, you can use these changes to spend less.

A survey— stop. Note on surveys: they are done by banks and insurance companies to make us buy stuff. That's not to say the results are not correct, useful or interesting. But you'll see what I mean in a minute. A survey by one particular insurance company published in May 2004 found that on average we each waste £1724 a year on uneaten food, unworn clothes, unplayed CDs, unsmelt perfume, unread books, abandoned hobbies, unused gadgets and unused travel tickets. The total waste – the average times the number of people over 16 – is an unimaginably huge £80 billion. Or as much as the government spends on defence, transport, agriculture, industry, housing, employment and the environment. And the insurance company's conclusion? Don't do it. Pay off your credit-card debt and spend the rest on savings products! Preferably from the company carrying out the survey. Which funnily enough is what most of us would do, the survey found, with the money we stopped wasting. But the strange thing is there is no mention of all the money we waste on financial products we don't need, commission we should not have paid, and bank charges and penalties. I wonder if they didn't ask. Or just ignored it.

So the next time you throw out a soggy lettuce (the biggest offender, apparently), you will be contributing to this mountain of wasted money. In your spending diary, why not have a little 'waste' column? 'Things I bought and never used.' And try to keep it down. And the survey? It was based on interviews with 1010 people in April 2004. They chucked away a lot of lettuce.

OK. We've looked at what comes in and what goes out and seen how to control what we spend. But in the revolving door that is our financial life, there are some things that go out that really shouldn't. So we are going to continue by taking our first baby steps towards getting our own back – from finance companies.

If you want to know what God thinks of money, just look at the people he gave it to.

Dorothy Parker

Chapter 3
Getting your own back

❏ Banks

❏ Bills

❏ Insurance

❏ Tax

t's time to examine banks. Look at the statements of your current account. On the income side will be your salary and perhaps child benefit or tax credits paid direct to your bank. Most of what you spend will be payments you have made with cheques, debit cards, standing orders, direct debits and cash withdrawals. But has your bank been picking your pocket? The essence of the pickpocket is (a) distraction (b) speed (c) stealth. The victim doesn't notice his money has gone until it's too late. Yes, we're talking bank charges.

■ Bank charges

Banks never send out bills. When you open a bank account there are pages of small print and you sign the form or click on the box on the internet and agree to it all. No one ever reads it. And if they do it is almost impossible to understand. So what is on your statement as an expense that you do not recognize? It may be called 'commission' or 'charges' or 'interest' and it will always be on the debit side – in other words, the money is coming out of your account. Without you knowing about it.

Is the balance in your account positive all month? In other words, do you never go overdrawn? What? You don't know how to tell? Look at your bank statement. All right, take it out of the bin and uncrumple it first. Now look at it. Are there any numbers with DR after them, as in £163.42DR? That is an amount taken out of your account. Or a balance you owe the bank. Money owed to the bank used to be in red. Hence 'I went into the red last month'. But progress being what it is, having two colour inks is too difficult today. So the banks put the letters DR after negative amounts. What does DR stand for? Well, CR means credit and stands for CreditoR. And DR stands for DebitoR. They're both Latin. It's all part of making things easy to understand. Though, to be fair, some banks do now use OD: OverDrawn.

Amazingly enough, there once was a man called Ralph M. DeBit who qualified as a medical practitioner and was therefore known as Dr DeBit. He died in 1992 at the age of 81. But he is not relevant to our story.

So – you never go overdrawn or into DR Debit country. Good. Now look at what you earn each month. Does the bank pay you any interest? Most High Street banks pay the derisory sum of 0.1 per cent. In other words, you have £1000 in the bank for a year and the bank gives you £1, first deducting 20p tax, which leaves you with 80p. Now compare that with owing the bank £1000. You would end up paying between £100 and £200. So you get 80p; the bank gets, say, £150. It's hardly fair. So it's time to get revenge. Leave your bank! A bank that pays 0.1 per cent interest does not deserve your business.

Moving is easy – more on that later – but where to go? Well, several banks do pay you a much better rate of interest than 0.1 per cent. You may have seen the adverts offering '20 times' normal interest. Well, even 20 times next to nothing is not great. But it is better than next to nothing. In fact, you can get far more than that. Here's what's on offer as I write this book. But in the wonderful world of interest rates, things change almost daily. So these are just examples and you must check the best deals before you go for one. Top for simple accounts just now is cahoot. It's online only but pays 3.93 per cent. So if you have £1000 in there on average throughout the year you get £39.30. Now the Chancellor won't let you earn that without taxing you, so that's £39.30 minus £7.86 tax, which leaves you with £31.44. That is £30.64 more than you would get with the major High Street banks. Or almost. Because Lloyds TSB currently have an even better offer, which will give you 4.89 per cent. But – of course, there is a but – you must have an income going into the account of at least £2000 a month. That means a salary of around £33,000 a year. But if this is a joint account and you are one of a couple, you each need a gross income of around £15,200. That doesn't seem so bad, does it? And even if you have the account all to yourself, you can get 4.25 per cent interest with a salary of around £15,200 – i.e. at least £1000 a month going into it. Another advantage is that the account has a special offer of 0 per cent overdrafts – as long as you arrange them in advance – until 30 August 2005. Then they revert to 17.9 per cent. That overdraft deal is only for new customers.

Now you might think this is a lot of fuss about nothing. If you don't have much in your current account, even at around 4 per cent the interest you earn will be very little. But this is the first baby step. Remember Mao. The longest journey starts with a single step. Even if it's £10 a year, it's better in your pocket than the bank's. Once a year buy a small round of drinks and think of your bank manager – not that you will ever have met her or him.

Look at it another way, you have a £10 note in your pocket. Someone nicks it. Do you shrug and say, 'It's only a tenner, why bother?' Or do you feel really pissed off, annoyed with yourself for being so careless? And furious with the thief who took it? That thief is your bank! Don't let it pick your pocket.

There's more. Perhaps in the past you have been encouraged to join an account like Lloyds TSB Gold Service, the Co-op's smilemore account or Barclays Additions. There are lots of these accounts and they charge you a fixed monthly fee, say between £2.50 and £12. At the time of writing you get very little for this fee– insurance products you may or may not need, and which you'd be better to choose yourself if you do. So if you see a small regular payment on your current account statement, change accounts now – £6 a month is £72 a year, £12 is £144. You could do something with that. You could even use it to make a standing order to your favourite charity. And get the Chancellor to boost your gift through gift aid – see Charity, page 64.

To find out which banks pay the best rates on current accounts, and which charge the least for overdrafts, check Follow-up (see page 200).

■ Online banking

A current account is not just about interest. It is about the quality of the service you get. If you are going to control your financial affairs, then you must convert either to an internet account – by far the best option – or at least to its older cousin, telephone banking.

With internet banking you can look at your account, move money around, check your balance and see what payments have come in and gone out 24 hours a day, 365 days a year. You can change payments, make payments, query amounts that have – or have not – been taken from or put into your account. You are in control. And if you are a bit reluctant to use the computer, almost all of them have a telephone helpline if you get stuck.

One of the great things about online banking is that you can easily get a list of your standing orders and direct debits – and cancel the old ones. It is a strange feature of direct debits that even when they stop being used, they stay on your bank account until *you* cancel them. So getting a list of them and cancelling the old ones is essential to controlling your money. Put the list in date order. And then see, day by day, how your pay will disappear. That will help you see how much you can afford at different times of the month.

If you don't have easy access to a computer and the internet – and if you have a dial-up account it will cost you money – then a telephone bank is nearly as convenient. But pick one with a genuine 24-hour, 365-day service. You never know, you might need to check your balance on Christmas Day.

The clearing system

When you use online banking you will notice one thing at once. Money still takes just as long to move from one bank to another. As soon as you hit the return key to send a payment, the money comes out of your account. But it still takes at least three and usually four or more days to arrive in the other bank. Where is it? It is in the infamous 'clearing system'. This was invented in the days when men in bowler hats carried cheques round the City from one bank to another. And it hasn't changed. It may seem reasonable to take three days to move money when a piece of paper has to be sent to the bank of the person you paid it to, passed on to your bank, checked against your account and finally deducted. But in the days of internet banking it seems plain daft.

Officially the 'clearing cycle' takes three days. But it is always longer. First, money can only move on a weekday. It just cannot be bothered to travel at all at the weekend, nor, of course, on a bank holiday. Also, in banking the day ends in the middle of the afternoon, around 4pm. Anything that happens after that doesn't happen until the next day. Then the bank that receives the money usually adds a day or two just to be sure it is not the victim of fraud. The result is that your money hangs around in what are called 'suspense accounts' (no, it's not because you are in suspense waiting for it to arrive) and the banks earn money by investing it overnight. Your money, their profit.

Of course, they can do it more quickly through another clearing system called CHAPS (the slow one is called BACS). If you have ever bought a house or paid for a car with a banker's draft, you will know that the money moves the same day. But they charge you for doing it – at least £25.

What with the profit on the overnight money and the profit banks make from CHAPS payments when things are really urgent, it is no surprise that the system stays one of the slowest in the civilized world.

Unfortunately, there isn't much to be gained in terms of transmission time by moving from one bank to another because they all use the same system. Though some of the newer banks and smaller building societies are even slower, none of the banks you use will be much quicker than the standard (roughly) four days between the money leaving one account and arriving in the other. All this can cost you money. If a credit card has to be paid by a certain date, or you want to avoid overdraft charges, always remember to leave a four-working-day margin for the banks to trundle your money in trolleys across the country.

Changing banks

Moving banks is easy. Once you have picked your new bank, you open the account and then tell your old bank. It has to tell your new bank about the standing orders and direct debits coming out of your account within five days and cooperate fully in your move to the new bank. The new bank can sometimes also sort out the money that goes into your account – from your employer, for example – although often you will have to do that bit. It might take three or four weeks to get it all sorted but it can be well worth it.

Wherever you bank, you can withdraw money from a cash machine at any bank without paying a charge. The machines normally display the Link logo. But beware. Some Link ones in small shops, garages, motorway service areas and even some post offices will make a charge, typically of around £1.50. It will always be shown on the screen before you take out your money. But usually it's timed so that although you *could* cancel, it's such a fuss that you pay up anyway. Pocket picked!

■ Household bills

Warmth, light and water. And to these we can now add chat and entertainment. Or to put all these costs more formally – utilities and communication. These are the regular bills that sap the strength of our bank accounts. Or do I mean 'zap'? Because that is what it feels like. You get paid on the 25th. And then *Zap!* Out goes the electricity charge. *Whoomph!* The gas bill burns a hole. *Ker-splash!* The water rates drain out. And then there's the mobile phone, the fixed-line phone, the satellite or cable TV, and that really neat ADSL connection for the computer. Plus £2 a month going to a charity somewhere that you signed up for outside W.H. Smith one day when you were waiting to meet a friend. Then there's your rent or mortgage, your gym subscription – you really *must* go more often – council tax, car payments, the loan for the sofa, your credit-card payments, and two or three things you've long since forgotten ever setting up. Then the bank helps itself to a few pounds for you know not what. And after that lot you have almost nothing left for the month. Your boss puts your pay into your bank account and all these other guys take it out! And you thought it was *your* money.

Let's get back to household stuff. We waste hundreds of millions of pounds a year between us by not spending a few minutes thinking about what we spend on electricity, gas and water.

Nearly ten years ago there was a revolution in Britain. You may have missed it. No one died and the government carried on. But in 1996 British Gas lost its monopoly to supply Britain with gas. And a couple of years later the local electricity companies began to lose their local monopolies too. It was one of those bold political ideas that actually worked. It brought down prices. And the revolution continues. Despite rising energy prices on the world markets, you can still usually save money by switching suppliers. On average – and this is a very broad average – you can save about £150 a year if you switch your gas and electricity supplier. Despite that, most people – about six out of ten of us – haven't switched. Nowadays a switch turns on savings rather than the lights!

The 'supplier' is really the company that charges you for what you use. You get the same gas through the same pipes and the same power through the same wires. It just costs less money. And if you are denying yourself that morning cappuccino to save a couple of pounds a day, where's the point in wasting £150 a year on essentials like keeping your home warm, your TV on and your beer cold?

In the past the problem was that customers were faced with a bewildering array of tariffs, and working out which was best for them was just about impossible. Today it has all been automated through a number of websites that enable you to put in your postcode and how much you spend on your gas or electricity in a year and then tell you which is the cheapest alternative. They will even let you click on a box and do all the paperwork online. Which is not quite as kind as it seems because, of course, the websites get commission for everyone who switches using their site. (See Follow-up, page 201.)

Websites will encourage you to take your gas and electricity from the same supplier (don't worry, the gas still comes through pipes and the electricity through the wires ...). These so-called 'dual fuel' deals may be the best. But then again they may not. So check out the price of electricity and gas separately as well, and if it's cheaper go with two different suppliers.

You also get a discount for paying by direct debit. Most suppliers prefer you to pay an estimated amount each month, and this is taken off your bill, which is still worked out every three months. Monthly payments suit most customers because most people get paid monthly. And it suits the suppliers because they get our money earlier and, if we pay a bit too much, they get to keep our money in their bank accounts earning interest.

So keep an eye on your bills and if you are still in credit in the winter, talk to your suppliers about paying a less each month. If you are out when the meter reader comes – aren't you always! – read your own and send the reading off to the company. That means you will be paying the right amount.

▉ GOLDEN RULE ON SWITCHING TARIFFS

■ Do it yourself over the internet, checking the information carefully

There are still horror stories about the techniques used by unscrupulous sales staff calling door-to-door to get people to switch tariffs. These salespeople trick customers into signing a form, often claiming they are simply reading the meter. Then, armed with a signature, the supplier in question switches the customer to its dual fuel tariff. Some of the more straightforward lies told include: 'Your supplier is no longer regulated. You need to switch to XX Electric.' 'Your electricity comes from France. Switch to a British supplier.' And my favourite: 'I am from energywatch. Can I look at your bills and save you money?' Never buy anything on the doorstep. If someone comes to the door, give them no information, sign nothing and send them away.

One day, while I was working quietly at home, the doorbell rang. I answered the door and a young man asked if I wanted to save money on my fuel bills. (It's hard to say no to that one.) He then showed me a page of supposed savings I'd make if I changed my supplier to his company. I asked if I could have a copy and think about it. He said he had none. When I asked for a number to call he said he couldn't give it to me. So I asked to see the sheet, which he handed to me. 'Can I go and copy it?' 'No,' he said, 'that's not allowed.' But it was too late. I was already walking to my study where I photocopied it. Moments later I returned to be told I had stolen his sheet and he would call the police. I gave it back to him, keeping the copy. 'That's still theft,' he said, and pulling out his mobile phone he called the police. I shut the door. A little while later a rather bemused police officer called round. I explained what had happened. I kept the copy. I didn't switch.

Water is different from gas or electricity. And not just because you can drink it. (Mind you, I had an uncle once ... but that's another story.) You cannot switch water supplier. Your water bill will still come from the local water company, which also provides the water and the pipes it runs through. The same company – or another – may be responsible for taking away waste water and sewage. You will normally get a bill once a year and the option of paying it in two or maybe 12 instalments. Again, direct debit often saves you money.

But there are bigger savings to be made. At the moment, water prices are still based on an obscure calculation related to how much your property could be rented out for in the dim and distant past. But since 2000 everyone has been able to change to paying for what they use. Switching to a water meter could cut your bill. Especially if you live alone or are economical with water. If you switch, then bills for both water and sewerage will be based on the volume of water that comes out of your taps. (Because the amount that goes down the drain and toilet is pretty much the same as what comes out of the taps. Think about it!) If the water you use is based on a meter, so is the water down the drain.

Almost everyone can have a meter fitted – the only exceptions may be some blocks of flats. Your local water company will fit one free, either inside or on the front or side wall of your home. The average annual cost of water and sewerage is £258 unmetered and £222 metered. A saving of £36 a year. Many people, especially those who live alone, will save much more than that. Some people, of course, will pay more with a meter. But you can change back any time within the first year if you find you're not saving. Contact your water company about getting a meter. The number will be on your bill.

■ Communication bills

It is a sign of the times that we spend more on chatting on the phone than we do on heating and lighting our homes. And that means there is scope for saving more money. If you thought gas and electricity tariffs were complicated, telephone tariffs make them look like two plus two. It is known as confusion marketing. It's designed to *offer* low prices but *charge* high ones.

There's a whole book to be written on minimizing phone bills. Here I will just go through some of the basics, starting with that 100-year-old marvel, the fixed-line phone. You know, the one attached to a wire which runs to a pole in the street down to a junction box then through a tunnel to the nearest exchange. Where, for all we know, ladies with permed hair still push jack plugs into a panel and silently say, 'Putting you through, caller.'

All those local copper wires and exchanges are still owned by British Telecom (BT), the private company that took over the telephones in the first privatization in 1984 (except in Hull, where the principle is the same but the charges are cheaper). And BT still dominates the market, despite numerous attempts at introducing real competition.

Golden – but useless – Rule of Telephone Calls: there is always a cheaper way to make any particular call. Finding out what it is and how to do it, however, is impossible. The best you can do is use a supplier that overall, for you, would be less costly. Probably.

Even BT has a tariff table that makes Stephen Hawking's blackboard look like a two-times table. Comparing that with all the others is like asking if eating a chocolate profiterole with cream will make you fatter than staying in bed for a week, eating toast and reading *War and Peace*. Never mind a Plain English award, what about a Clear Numbers prize? Perhaps I should sponsor one.

BT called me the other day (because, no, I haven't switched myself) and asked if I was happy on my tariff because they had brought out a new one and it might be cheaper for me. 'For me?' I asked. Well, no. Generally. Many customers would find it a cheaper and more convenient tariff. What was my pattern of calls? I replied that my pattern of calls tended to be that when I wanted to speak to someone I picked up the phone and did so. And I wasn't terribly aware that I did so at particular times or that my friends and family lived in particular number areas. But, BT insisted, did I use the phone often during the day? Yes. More than in the evenings and at weekends? I didn't know. But then I had a bright idea. It was BT after all. 'Tell you what,' I said. 'You know what my bill is and what my pattern of calls is because you send me a list of them every three months. Why don't you run the last three months calls through your computer and see if the new tariff would save me money?' 'I'm sorry, sir, I don't have that information here due to Data Protection rules. Is there anything else I can help you with at this time?' There wasn't.

There are three ways to save money on your BT calls. But first here is one very simple way to save money if you have a mobile phone. If you are at home and want to call someone on the same mobile network as you, use the mobile to make the call rather than the fixed phone, because it will be cheaper than BT. Always. BT charges a scandalous amount to call mobile phones. Similarly, if you want to call someone from your mobile who has a mobile on the same network as you, call them on that, not on their fixed line. Mobile networks charge a scandalous amount to call fixed lines and, come to that, other mobile networks.

Back to BT and those three ways of saving money. The easiest is to use an alternative phone company through what is known as 'carrier pre-select'. That phrase is not quite as meaningless as it sounds. It means you choose (select) in advance (pre-) the company that will carry your calls (carrier). By law, BT has to honour this choice and sets up its exchange so that all calls from your number use that other carrier. Some alternative carriers offer free calls if they are made at certain times of the day or to other people using their service; others make a fixed charge. Some are better for international calls;

others for UK calls. You get two bills: one from BT for the line rental (and you are in BT's hands here because that may go up) and the other from the carrier you have chosen for your calls. But the overall cost will usually be cheaper than sticking with BT.

If you prefer, you can use other providers for just some of your calls, in which case you dial a four- or five-digit code before the number, and the call then goes with the other supplier. You still pay BT for your line rental and, of course, for any calls when you do not dial an access code. In theory you could choose the supplier that was cheapest for particular calls and have a whole list of access codes by the phone. It may be the best way to save the most money. But could you be bothered?

About one BT customer in three has changed to another carrier for some of their calls. No one knows how much can be saved by switching to another supplier, although one of the carrier pre-select companies claims that 22 million BT customers could save £42 a year each by switching. If you have your phone bills to hand, know who you call and when, and can log on to a website (see Follow-up, page 201), you can get an estimate of the cheapest way to make your calls. And if you try it and don't like it, you can always switch back just as easily.

The third way is to stick with BT, get a copy of its tariffs and then give Professor Hawking a call. Because BT won't help you. For a practical alternative, see Follow-up, page 201. Oh, and pay by direct debit. It's cheaper that way.

Mobile phones

Even more complex than fixed-line tariffs are the ones charged by mobile phones. Having used the Stephen Hawking gag for BT call charges, I'm not sure where to go with a description of how abstruse mobile phone tariffs are. But I doubt even the Lucasian Maths Prof at Cambridge could write a formula that took your details and produced the best-fit mobile-call tariff. Call charges make event horizon equations look like GCSE maths. There, I knew I'd find one.

The best way to save money is to use your mobile less. And text less. Text messages can cost a fortune. In 2003 we sent just over 20 billion of them. At 10p a time that's £2 billion of revenue for mobile phone companies. 'Err, excuse me,' I hear you say, 'mine don't cost me 10p. I get them free with my monthly plan.' Sorry? You get them free? In exchange for money? What definition of 'free' does that come under? If you look at the cost, they are about 5p each if you buy a set number a month – you pay for those whether you use them or not. After that they are 10p each. They are never free.

Sending pictures is even more expensive. 25p a time with some companies. OK, it's only the price of posting a letter, and it gets there a lot quicker. But how often do you send a letter to your friends with a picture of you in that little bar on the beach sticking your tongue out?

A pre-pay phone costs much more per call than one where you get a monthly bill. And more per message: in some cases as much as 12p for text, and 30p for a picture. So shift to a monthly bill. It will save you money. If you are already on a monthly bill, order an itemized one – but check first whether it's free. (Some companies now charge you for the privilege of telling you how they worked out what you owe them.) Put your left brain in gear and study who you call, when and what it costs. Log on to your network's website and see if you can save money by changing tariffs. If you are an Orange customer, then Orange will do the work for you if you call into one of their shops with a few of your phone bills. And there is one website that helps you choose the best mobile tariff (see Follow-up, page 201). But I am going to leave this one to you. Partly because I know that whatever I say you will use that little magic handset whenever you want to have a chat. And just pay up.

TV

Your television is another thing that can waste money. We all have to pay the TV licence – unless someone aged 75 or more lives in the house, in which case the licence is free.But beyond that there is money to be saved if you pay for Sky or a cable service. Take Sky. Hundreds of channels, but how many do you watch? And of those, how many do you pay extra for? Films are expensive and so is sport. If you could cut out either of these you would save £6 or £7 a month. If you cut out both you could save £20 a month, and if you cut out still more channels you could end up paying just £13.50 a month. Write down how many of the movie or sport channels you watch each month and for how long, and see what it's costing you. Then decide if it is worth spending £480 a year for them when you can pay a great deal less.

Similar savings can be made with cable channels. And, of course, you can save all this money by buying a Freeview box for about £60 which gives you a range of digital widescreen channels for nothing. (But you might have to buy a new aerial to receive it and it is not available everywhere in the UK.)

As with telephones and utilities, confusion marketing is used to make all these choices difficult. Try finding out the cost of a basic Sky service on its website! Sky and cable will also throw in cheap telephone calls or broadband access, but untangling these offers is deliberately made difficult. The only general rule is: Think about it before you sign up. And if you are already signed up, think what you are really getting with the money you spend.

■ Getting your own back

Waste. Stuff that drains away money on things that are not necessary and not even fun in the first place. Do we need all the insurance we have accumulated? How can we get rid of it? Are we paying too much tax – to the Chancellor or the local council? How do we stop the rot?

It is one of the truisms of the financial services industry that insurance is sold, not bought. In other words, no one in their right mind would rush out on a Saturday morning and say: 'Gosh, I must find a shop to sell me insurance.' That could be for several reasons. It is very boring. It is hard to understand. It protects against things we really really hope will not happen. It is not worth having. Often it's all four.

I am not the world's biggest fan of insurance, or what the industry is now trying to rebrand 'protection'. We really have to ask: What does it protect you against? How likely is that to happen? And what if it does? So looking at insurance and avoiding it wherever possible is a very good way of keeping more money to spend on important things. Like savings, pensions and shoes.

■ Life insurance

One insurance company estimated recently that we are £2 billion under-insured on life insurance. I think it is equally likely that we are £2 billion over-insured. Because life insurance is not just sold, it is secretly sold. We accumulate insurance policies every time we take out a pension, endowment policy, mortgage, loan, or any other insurance against illness or unemployment. Now there are circumstances in which life insurance is a vital and valuable product. If you have dependants, then you naturally want to make sure as far as you can that your sudden or unexpected death would not leave them with financial problems. But always remember: the objective of insurance salespeople is not to protect us, but to earn easy commission from what can seem very cheap products.

> We are born with nothing. So if we die in debt we are ahead.
>
> *Paul Lewis 2001*

Do you need life insurance at all? If you have no dependants, the answer is simply no. A single person who is not a parent and who doesn't have a joint mortgage with anyone does not need life insurance. And do not believe the sales spiel that goes like this: 'If you died, you wouldn't want your relatives to have to pay off your debts, would you?' No one has to pay your debts when you die. The money from items in your estate – property, possessions, savings and so on – is added up, and any debts are paid from that. If your debts are more than your estate, no one has to pay the balance. Many advisers don't seem to know this. One company tried to market a life insurance product to cover debts and 'give your relatives peace of mind' if you died. And the boss of one financial services company wrote to *Financial Adviser* in July 2004 to say: 'If a single person had died while in negative equity [owing more on their mortgage than their home was worth], their family would have had to find the difference.' Not true. But widely believed, apparently, by the people who sell, and buy, life insurance.

If you have dependants, what will they need if you die? Children are the first consideration. And here you probably need what is called 'term assurance'. This is a cheap product that replaces your income until your youngest child is independent, say at 21. Next comes your spouse. Nowadays, husbands and wives lead more independent financial lives than they used to and penury does not always follow the death of one partner. There is one thing, however, that does need protecting. Your home. If you have a mortgage with someone else it is vital that if one of you dies before it is paid off, there is insurance to repay the debt in full. Otherwise the other person may face the prospect of having to sell the property to repay the loan – homeless, as well as bereaved. If you have an endowment mortgage, the amount you pay each month will already include life insurance to repay the loan if one of you dies. And many people with a repayment mortgage will also have been sold life insurance when they took it out. But make sure that the amount you have insured does not form part of your estate. If it does, and you leave more than £263,000, inheritance tax will be due. The way to avoid this is to arrange your policy to be 'written in trust' so that the money is left in trust and then used to repay the mortgage. You can arrange this at the time you take it out or later. Ask the insurance company – it shouldn't cost you anything.

What other life insurance you might need is something you should discuss with your dependants. First, look at what insurance you already have. If you belong to a company pension scheme you probably have life insurance, often as much as three times your annual salary. That might be enough.

Cancelling unnecessary life cover can save you money. The unnecessary sale of life cover comes back to commission – the sales agent can get more than two years' premiums up front and 2.5 per cent of your annual premiums for the rest of your life.

■ Critical illness insurance

As if that were not enough, salespeople will try to sell you other insurance along with your life insurance. They may well tell you there is more chance of illness or disability than death. Which, if you think about it, is clearly nonsense. Critical illness cover has become very popular. A million policies were sold in 2002, and around five million people have this cover. It is usually sold with other insurance, especially if you're buying a home or are self-employed. Typically it will cost around £30 a month and will promise £100,000 if you get one of seven major health problems, including cancer and heart disease. It sounds useful. But the price is going up and the criteria for claiming are becoming ever stricter. Some cancers are now excluded and some companies will only pay out after your second heart-bypass operation. In other words, take it out now and by the time you need it you'll find that the premiums you paid for many years were a waste of money. Don't buy it. If you have it, think about cancelling it. Did I mention that commission rates are very high on this? I didn't need to, really, did I? But the salesperson can keep up to half your premiums for up to four years! That may earn them £2000 for one sale.

A better deal for you – which is why it pays much less commission – is called permanent health insurance or PHI. PHI pays out if disability or illness prevents you from working, which is much more likely than getting one of the 'dread diseases' that critical illness policies insure against. PHI replaces up to 75 per cent of your income, though some insurers are now reducing this to 60 per cent. Before considering it, check what your employer will pay – many will give full pay for six months and half pay for another six months. The cost of the insurance can be reduced by deferring the period before the insurance starts by up to 52 weeks and there is no point in paying for cover when your employer will pay up anyway. Some policies will only pay up if you are incapable of doing any work, not just your normal job, which is a tough condition to meet. If your disability turns out to be permanent the insurance will pay you until you reach a certain age, between 50 and 65. The premiums will get more expensive as you get older.

▓ Insurance to scrap

Extended warranties are no such thing. They are a form of insurance that covers the cost of repairs if an electrical item stops working properly, and they are never worth having. The commission rates drive the market – people who sell you goods earn as much again or more if they sell you this insurance too.

> I went to my local electrical retailers to buy a fridge. After considering the options, and with the help and encouragement of the salesman, I eventually decided which one to buy. A new frost-free fridge that was economical and reliable. The salesman then asked if I wanted breakdown insurance. 'No,' I said. 'But this is new technology,' he insisted. 'It may need repairing and you would be faced with the loss of everything in it.'

I repeated, 'No thanks.' He persisted, 'Why not?'

'You sold it to me for convenience and reliability. Now you are telling me the chances are it will go wrong within a couple of years. I don't want it. Thanks.' He went to get the manager. Similar questions from him. The same answers from me. The manager: 'Right, John, Mr Lewis has made it clear he does not want that insurance. Write it on the receipt in case of dispute later.' I still have the receipt. And the fridge. In ten years it has never gone wrong.

All goods are covered by retail laws that effectively guarantee them for a year. Some stores will guarantee them for longer. Research by the Consumers Association shows extended warranties are generally a waste of money – modern appliances are very reliable and unlikely to break down within five years. Sales of this kind of insurance are not regulated and the people selling it do not have to be trained or qualified to sell insurance.

Equally bad is credit-card protection. If your cards are lost or stolen you are not liable for anything bought on them as long as you took reasonable care and tell the card company swiftly. So you are being asked to pay to insure someone else's risk. Pocket picked!

Ditto payment protection cover, which will always be offered to you when you take out a loan, a credit card or a mortgage. It is normally sold as 'protecting your payments if you fall ill or lose your job'. Which is not true. These products do not pay out in many circumstances and do not necessarily cover all your payment for the length of the loan. They can double the cost of a bank loan (see page 122) and are usually a waste of money. The only people who get peace of mind from them are those who sell them – they get a guaranteed cut as long as you pay the premiums.

Private health insurance is essential in countries where there is no free health service. But not in the UK. Because here you are buying not valuable health care but better health care than the NHS will provide. So you are buying a shorter wait for non-urgent treatment, a private room, perhaps a sense of getting special care. But if you have an acute medical problem, the chances are the same people will look after you as if you went to the NHS, the same surgeon will operate, often in the same building. You should also consider that the premiums get higher and higher as you get older. So when you reach the age when treatment becomes more likely, you may find you can't afford to pay them.

So my money-saving tip is simple. Put the money you would have spent on the premiums into a separate savings account – call it 'health' or 'medicine' if you like. If you need treatment for a painful, but non-urgent, condition, use the money to buy private care if it will speed things up or improve the attention you get. Many private hospitals will offer guaranteed prices on common operations. But let the NHS take care of the rest. And leave private health care to the people who pay ten times as much to cross the Atlantic – and get there no quicker than the rest of us do in the back of the plane.

▉ Tax drag

Tax is not something any of us likes paying, so the government has devised ways over the years to make it as painless as possible. Tax is taken off our earnings before we are paid. And it is normally automatically deducted from the interest our savings earn. Automatic deductions like this are convenient for the government because they guarantee the tax is collected. Unfortunately, the system doesn't guarantee that the amount of tax taken off us is correct.

In 2000, the Inland Revenue estimated that it had taken £300 million too much tax off four million people with savings. No one knows how much is overcharged on tax that is deducted from wages, but some accountants' estimates suggest this happens in one case out of ten. You may be paying too much tax and never know it. Unless you check – and, sadly, that is not easy.

PAYE is the dull name given to the automatic deduction of tax from our wages. It stands for Pay As You Earn. Each year we can have £4745 of income before tax is due. Depending whether you are paid monthly or weekly, the Inland Revenue divides that 'tax allowance' into 12 or 52 and spreads it over the year. So if you are paid monthly you get £395 of income untaxed, and if you are paid weekly it's about £91 untaxed – the rest is taxed. Your employer works it all out using what is called a 'tax code', which is normally 474L. The 474 means you can have £4749 untaxed income (the 5 is rounded up to a 9), and the L means nothing really, though it used to. If your tax code is anything else, your tax is being treated in a special way. If you have a BR code or an 0T code, it means that all your income from that job is being taxed with no tax-free allowance, in which case you should find out what's going on!

If you have a spell out of work during the tax year, you may end up paying too much tax. If you work for ten months, for example, and then don't work for the next two months, you will only have had 10 x £395 = £3950 income tax-free, instead of £4745. So you will be due back the tax you have paid on the balance, which will be £175. If you think you might be in this position, contact your local Inland Revenue Enquiry Centre and ask how to get your tax checked and any refund paid.

■ Spending that can reduce your tax

If you travel around as part of your job, your employer can refund you your car-travel costs and no tax is due on that money. If you make the journeys in your own car, you can be paid up to 40p a mile without that money counting as part of your pay, so no tax or National Insurance is due on it. And it gets better. Suppose your employer is a bit mean and instead of 40p a mile pays you only 25p. You drive 1000 miles in your own car on errands for work. Your employer pays you £250, which is tax-free. And you can claim tax relief on another £150. In other words, you do not need to pay tax on £150 of your income, which is worth £33. So at the end of the tax year claim that £33 back from the Inland Revenue. If you are an employee, you should contact the tax office that deals with your employer. Your pay office can tell you which one that is. Or contact your Inland Revenue Enquiry Centre.

You may also be able to claim a small tax allowance for the upkeep of tools you use for your job, or for the upkeep and cleaning of a uniform you wear. These allowances are worth just a few pounds a year. But baby steps! Better in your pocket than in the Chancellor's. You can find out more from your Inland Revenue Enquiry Centre.

Some employees can claim an allowance if they have to join a professional society or subscribe to a journal. Ask your employer, or any professional society you belong to, whether you can claim the cost and reduce your tax bill.

Charity

Do you give to charity? If so, do you make sure that the Chancellor gives too? Every time you give a pound to charity the Chancellor will add 28p. But only if you do it right. It's called gift aid. And it is very simple. You just have to sign a declaration that you are a UK taxpayer. It doesn't matter what rate of tax you pay as long as you pay at least as much tax as the amount you give to charity in the year. That makes it a Gift, with a big G, and the charity then asks the Chancellor to chip in his 28 penn'orth. So you write a cheque for £100 and the charity ends up with £128.21.

If you are a higher-rate taxpayer – three million of us are – then it gets better. Because when you fill in your self-assessment form, you can claim back the rest of the tax you have paid on your donation and that comes off your tax bill. It's a slightly tricky calculation, but you can claim back 23p for every £1 you gave. So if you have given £100, you can claim £23.08 off your tax. So while the charity has got £128.21, it has only cost you £76.92. Or you can also give the £23.08 to the charity, by ticking a box on your tax form.

Tax on savings

If you have savings that are earning interest – and if your savings and bank accounts are *not* earning interest, and a good rate at that, read Savings, page 153 – then you will see from your statements that tax is taken off the interest automatically. Every month or year you will see a pair of entries that look something like this

Interest paid		£12.50
Tax on interest	£2.50	

In other words, your savings have earned £12.50 interest, and the bank has passed on £2.50 to the Inland Revenue, leaving you with £10. Now that's fine if you pay tax at the basic rate. The correct tax has been paid as painlessly as possible. It is a useful wheeze for the government. But not everyone should pay tax. Students, children, pensioners, parents who don't do paid work, low earners and many others normally have an income low enough to mean they don't have to pay tax. Nevertheless, automatic tax deduction means that millions of people who have an income too low to pay tax on have, in fact, been taxed. An even better wheeze for the government!

Remember, each year we are all allowed a certain level of income before any tax is due. In 2004–2005 it is £4745 for most people (higher if you are blind or over 65). And if your income is more than this but up to £6765 you only have to pay tax on the difference (up to £2020) at 10 per cent. But the bank will still deduct tax from your interest at 20 per cent.

In 2000 the Inland Revenue estimated that four million low-income earners had paid £300 million in tax that should never have been deducted. Four years later, it has launched a few, rather lacklustre, campaigns to make people aware of this. But it cannot – or will not – say how successful they have been. 'Not very' is the most likely answer. So you should make sure your savings are not being wrongly taxed. There are two things you can do.

If you are not a taxpayer now, you can fill in a form called R85, which means that the bank or building society has to pay your interest without taking off the tax, or 'gross' as they like to call it. (I think the thing that's 'gross' is wrongly taking all that money off people!) Anyway, you get this form from either your bank or building society, or by contacting the Inland Revenue (see Follow-up, page 202).

If you think you should pay tax at the lower rate, or you think you've paid too much tax in previous tax years – and you can go back up to six previous tax years – then you need to fill in form R40. If you want to do that, the Inland Revenue insists you fill in one R40 for each tax year you are claiming for – which could be up to seven forms. You can get the forms from the Inland Revenue (see Follow-up, page 202); make sure you ask for enough.

■ Capital gains tax and inheritance tax

Two taxes cause a lot of fear, though hardly anyone has to worry about them: capital gains and inheritance tax. The Scylla and Charybdis of the tax system. But only the wealthiest and most adventurous need ever encounter them.

In the dim and distant past there was a way of avoiding tax used by wealthy people. Instead of taking an honest income from their savings by way of interest or dividends, they had their advisers devise products that did not produce an income but which grew in value. If you organized your finances in the right way or were wealthy enough to pay an adviser to do it for you, it was possible to sell these growing investments regularly and produce a steady stream of money that was not technically an 'income' and thus avoided income tax. In 1965, the new Labour Chancellor Jim Callaghan introduced a tax on this growth in your money. Capital gains tax (CGT) was born.

CGT has always been a minor player, bringing in relatively little money and affecting very few people. But it is a useful bogeyman for the financial services industry, who will add it to the list of taxes you are avoiding through some scheme or other, even though the chances of ordinary mortals paying it are remote.

That's partly because of three major concessions. First, the home you live in is exempt. So even if you sell it for a lot more than you bought it for, there is normally no tax to pay. Sorry about the 'normally'. But this exemption does not apply at all to a second home. And if you have a garden that's bigger than half a hectare – about one and a quarter acres – you might have to pay some CGT on the gain you make, even on your only home.

Second, you are allowed to make gains in one year of £8200 and pay no tax on them. That will cover most normal activities. Especially as husbands and wives get that allowance each.

Third – or rather third (a) – the longer you've owned the stuff before you sell it, the less tax there is to pay anyway. The tax is reduced for each year you've owned it since April 1998. After ten years the tax is 60 per cent of the full tax. And third (b), you can reduce the price you sold it for by the rate of inflation for each year you owned it before 1998.

That's a brief guide. You can see why accountants have so much to do! But as a result of these concessions, it's hardly a surprise that barely 150,000 people a year pay CGT: about 1 in 200 taxpayers. And it only brings in around £1.25 billion a year – barely 1 per cent of the money we pay in income tax.

Paying inheritance tax (once called 'death duties') is also a minority sport. Again it was a child of a Labour government and was originally intended to stop wealthy people avoiding death duties by handing over their wealth to their children before they died. It has been radically changed over the years – including the name change to inheritance tax (IHT) in 1986 – and now brings in a slightly more respectable £2.5 billion a year, but from only 32,000 estates. When you consider that 612,000 people died in 2003, that means 19 out of 20 estates escape inheritance tax – most because they are too small, but some because a married person dies and leaves everything to their spouse, in which case the money is completely exempt.

Both these taxes are a bit like crime – the fear of them does more damage than the reality. So if a financial adviser tries to sell you a scheme to avoid either of these taxes or an investment on the grounds that it helps avoid them, be very cautious. Unless you are one of the wealthiest 0.5 per cent in the country or you expect to die among the wealthiest 5 per cent, they are not going to be a problem.

At least, that's what the figures show. But inheritance tax is a growing problem for one simple reason: the amount we can leave free of tax goes up by about 3 per cent a year, but the value of our houses and flats is going up by about 20 per cent a year. At the moment inheritance tax is charged on the value of an estate above £263,000. The largest asset when most people die is their home, and the average price of that is around £160,000. Still well short of the tax level. But in many parts of the country, those nice homes our parents own – you know, the bigger ones in the nicer places, built when a bedroom was considerably bigger than a bed – are worth more than the average. In some parts of the UK, these homes are already above the inheritance-tax threshold.

So now I'm going to let you in on a little secret. It is the only safe, legal and guaranteed way for most people to avoid paying IHT on the family home. Well, of course, *you* won't have to pay it anyway. You'll be dead. But it's a way to avoid your loved ones finding that the taxman has taken a big chunk out of what you have left them. It's not a plan. Not a trick. But a perfectly practical step that is completely legal and that the government has said will not be changed. Unfortunately it only really works for married couples, and it only applies to your home. But that is the asset most likely to cause problems. If you have assets of £263,000 or more apart from your home, you can afford an accountant and I suggest you get one.

Deep breath. Horsehair wig on …

COUNSEL: There are, m'lud, two ways of owning a home. Way number one is as what we lawyers like to call 'joint tenants'. [*Interruption*]

JUDGE: Silence! For the benefit of the people in the public gallery who appear restless, I will explain at this point that when Mr erm, Mr erm, Mr Counsel, uses the phrase 'joint tenants' he is fully cognizant of the fact that you, in fact, own rather than rent your property. 'Joint tenants' is a legal phrase describing *how* you own it. Proceed. [*Interruption*] It may in your view be silly and, as I believe your friend shouted, confusing, but that is how the law is. Now be silent or I will clear the gallery. Mr Counsel.

COUNSEL: Thank you, m'lud. As you say, m'lud, two people – a couple, if you will – can own a property together in two ways. Normally they will own it as 'joint tenants', or as my learned Scottish friends would say, 'joint owners with survivorship'. In this case, in a sense, m'lud, they both own all the property. So when one dies the ownership simply passes to the other without formality. Alternatively they can own the property as what we like to call 'tenants in common'.

JUDGE: And in Scotland, Mr Counsel?

COUNSEL: I was about to say, in Scotland, m'lud, where you do not have jurisdiction, it is known simply as 'joint owners'. [*Interruption from the public gallery*]

JUDGE: No, I do not accept that the Scottish terminology is more sensible. It may be easier to understand but that is different. Very different. Mr Counsel.

COUNSEL: Now when property is owned as 'tenants in common', each party owns a clearly defined share. It may be 50 per cent each. Or, in fact, any other share such as 60:40, 75:25—

JUDGE: Yes, yes get on with it, we don't need more examples.

COUNSEL: But normally 50:50, or, m'lud, in the vernacular, half each. The difference between the two ways of joint ownership is important. A couple who own their property as 'tenants in common' can each leave their share in their will to their heirs. So when the first dies, half the home is left to the children who in their kindness and wisdom allow the surviving parent to remain in the home. When the grim reaper pays a second call, then that individual's share is also left to the heirs. In that way IHT is likely to be mitigated.

JUDGE: Would you care to explain how, with the help of this blackboard? It only has some scribbles by Stephen Hawking on it. The duster is on the side.

COUNSEL [with chalk]: Suppose the home is worth £500,000. Jane and John Suburban own the property as 'joint tenants'. John dies. Jane becomes owner of whole house. An estate which passes to a spouse is exempt from IHT so no tax is due. [*Public gallery: 'Hooray!'*] A year later Jane dies. House is now worth £510,000 and, together with other property, the total is £514,010. £514,010 minus £263,000 equals £251,010, which is taxed at 40 per cent. IHT due is £100,404. [*Sounds of booing from public gallery*]

JUDGE: Silence. Or I will clear the gallery. Mr Counsel.

COUNSEL: But suppose John and Jane Suburban had read this book! And changed the way they owned their home to 'tenants in common each owning 50 per cent'? John dies and leaves his half to the children together with £1000 and his collection of football programmes from the 1950s. Total estate £251,010. Well below the IHT limit. No IHT payable. [*Restless murmurings from the gallery: 'Just the same as last time.'*] The other half remains in the ownership of his wife. Sadly, within a year Jane also dies. Her half now passes to the heirs, total value £263,000, still just below the IHT limit. Result: no tax payable then either. [*Gasps, followed by cheers and stamping*]

JUDGE: Mr Counsel. Am I given to understand that a simple change of ownership saves more than £100,000 in tax?

COUNSEL: Yes, m'lud. [*The gallery is on its feet, waving and shouting*]

JUDGE: And how much was the book in which this advice is found?

COUNSEL: £7.99, m'lud.

JUDGE: £7.99? That is barely the price of a gin and tonic at my club. It is the finest bargain that has been before my court for twenty years. You know me of old, Mr Counsel, and my view is that twenty years should mean twenty years. Right to appeal refused. Take the Chancellor down to the cells and make him whistle for his £100,000 inheritance tax!

USHER: All rise!

Outside the court an excited crowd mobs Mr Counsel. 'How do we change the ownership of our home? How do we become thingies in common?'

But Mr Counsel is in no mood to give free advice. He is off, in a blur of black. So I will stand in as his clerk. All you need do is write a letter to each other saying that the property known as 3 Acacia Avenue currently owned by Jane and John Suburban as joint tenants will in future be owned by John and Jane Suburban as tenants in common in equal shares. You can also register this change of ownership at the Land Registry. In Scotland you should see a lawyer.

There are dangers. All the heirs are joint owners of the home and any of them could insist it be sold at any time. If any of them divorces or goes bankrupt then the courts could order the house to be sold to realize their share. And if any of them wanted to claim income support or help with their rent or council tax, owning a share of the home could prevent them from doing so. But that apart, if you are a married couple and you own a house worth more than £263,000, it is cast-iron guaranteed to save your heirs IHT.

■ Council tax

I hate to spoil the party, but council tax is something anyone with a home to live in has to pay. We don't like it. We wonder what we get for it. But we have to pay it or go to jail. But did you know that loads of people pay too much?

- If you live alone, or you are the only adult in the household (students do not count as adults – can't think why!), then you can get a 25 per cent discount.
- If you have a disability adaptation to your home, council tax is cut by around 17 per cent.
- If you have a lowish income and savings, you can get your council tax cut – to nothing in some cases.

Ask your local council. (See also Follow-up, page 202.)

There are people who have money and people who are rich.

Coco Chanel

Chapter 4
Rhythm of life

❑ Children

❑ Students

❑ Buying a home

❑ Reaching fifty

Throughout our lives we pass through stages – childhood, studying, work, relationships, buying a home, reaching 50, retiring. Each stage has its own issues and needs its own approach. This chapter looks at these rhythms of life. The next chapter looks at the spiky bits.

■ Children

To begin at the beginning, there are two sorts of children. Boys and girls. Good and bad. Those born before September 2002 and those born later. That dividing line separates children into two groups.

The younger children – born on 1 September 2002 or later – can have much more money saved up tax-free for them. They can have what is called a child trust fund (CTF). These funds grow tax-free and are given a kick-start at birth with a £250 gift from the Chancellor. Yes, I *did* say the Chancellor. He's really a very nice man. Another gift, probably of a similar size, will be paid when the child reaches the age of seven. Parents, grandparents, relatives, friends – indeed anyone – can put extra money into the CTF. The only restriction is that between them they cannot put in more than £1200 each tax year. The whole lot is given to the child when they are 18, and over the years the money can really mount up. And although parents may hope the child will use it to pay for university or as a deposit on their first home, there will be nothing to stop them throwing a party, buying a car or travelling round the world.

There are various sorts of CTF. Some will be like a savings account; others will be invested partly on the stock market. The parent has to choose which sort of CTF their child has. With an investment over this sort of period, that decision can be difficult. My preference would be for a good cash savings account. This has two advantages.

1. There will be no risk that there will be less money at the end than at the beginning. With a stock-market investment, even over 18 years, you will always have that risk. And on average the money saved up in a CTF account will be there for less than nine years. It is what I call a medium-term investment (see pages 151–2).

2. There will be no charges – it will be just like a savings account or a cash ISA for children. But if the CTF is invested rather than saved, then charges will be deducted. Some CTFs will charge an upfront fee – perhaps 5 per cent of every new amount of money paid in – plus an annual fee that could be as much as 2 per cent a year of the total value of the fund. The government has recognized the concern about these charges and some CTFs will be given the 'stakeholder' brand, whereby they will charge no upfront fee and no more than 1.5 per cent a year of the fund. No more than 60 per cent of the money will be at risk on the stock market – the rest will be in slightly less risky investments – and as the age of 18 approaches the fund will have to shift the balance of investment away from the stock market to avoid the risk of it losing a lot of value just before it's time to cash it in.

Let's see how the money might grow. Remember the government puts in £250 at birth – and double that if the child's parents have a joint income of less than £13,480 a year. There will be another present from the Chancellor at age seven. Let's assume that it's the same. If no one puts any more in and this money is in a savings account earning 4 per cent with no charges, by the age of 18 it will be worth £891. Not a lot really. But suppose generous relatives do chip in and between them each year the maximum of £1200 is put in. Then the total will be just three quid short of £33,000. Which by 2020 might be just about enough to see the little angel through university!

So for children born this side of the line, a child trust fund will be a handy place for any birthday or Christmas money to be saved up. And it will undoubtedly encourage saving – if not by them, then by their relatives.

Children's savings accounts

Children born before 1 September 2002 will not be able to have a CTF, but will have to make do with an ordinary old savings account instead – and, of course, they will not get the £250 gift from the Chancellor.

Parents and grandparents can still save up for them. But beware, the pickpockets are out again – this time offering distractions in the form of free gifts and cuddly toys while making off with your cash.

■ GOLDEN RULE OF SAVING FOR KIDS

■ Avoid any account that has the label 'children' or is named after a cuddly animal

Most accounts branded specially for children are poor value. They often come with free gifts ranging from the traditional moneybox to vouchers for CDs. But you pay for these 'gifts' because the rates of interest are usually not as good as those in the best standard savings accounts, which you can always open for a child. If you want to tie the money up for a year or more, you would do better to buy a fixed-rate bond, which can pay up to 6 per cent over four or five years.

One person who will not steal your child's money is the Chancellor – as long as you remember to remind him. Tax is normally taken automatically off any interest earned. But if the parent fills in form R85, saying it is an account for a child who is not a taxpayer, then the interest is paid gross. However, there is a trap for the unwary. If the child's account earns interest of more than £100 a year on money given to them by a parent, then the whole of the interest is taxable as the parent's income, not the child's. The rule applies separately to money given by fathers and mothers. So if Dad puts £2000 into an account for a new baby at 4.75 per cent it will earn £95 a year interest and that will not be taxed. If Mum also does the same, that will not be taxed either. But if only one of them gives the whole £4000 then the interest will all be taxed as theirs.

This tax rule applies only to interest on money given by parents. The interest earned on money given to a child by anyone else, including grandparents, is treated as the child's income and is not normally taxed – unless the child is lucky enough to have an income above the personal tax allowance, currently £4745 a year.

Many friendly societies and insurance companies offer special stock market-based investments – often named after furry animals – for young savers. But charges can be high, conditions can be inflexible and investment performance has often been terrible. They are best avoided.

If the account is in the child's name then at a certain age they will be able to take control of it themselves. With a savings account, that age is usually between 7 and 11, although the child will normally have to be about 12 before banks and building societies will be happy to let them withdraw cash without parental supervision. The age is 16 for some products from National Savings & Investments, including the children's bonus bond, which, as I write, pays 4.7 per cent a year if held for five years. Children can't own shares until they reach 18 (16 in Scotland), so an investment in a shares-based fund has to be opened by an adult in their own name but 'designated' as the child's account. That in effect creates what is legally called a 'bare trust', whereby the adult controls the investment on the child's behalf until he or she reaches 18 – or 16 in Scotland.

■ Students

When I was at university, student debt meant leaving college with a £200 overdraft. Now, students leave university with frightening debts. In 2003–2004 the average was £12,069. And from 2006 onwards it will be worse. A total of £14.6 billion is currently owed by students from England and Wales to the Student Loans Company. The class graduating in 2009 will probably owe twice as much. But there is one good thing about student debt. It's cheap. Interest is added on each year, but only at the rate of inflation. In effect, the debt never gets bigger in real terms, and in terms of prices, it stays the same. So if a loaf of bread costs 60p this year and you owe £6000 – which will buy you 10,000 loaves of bread – and then prices rise over the years so that a loaf of bread costs £1.20, you will owe £12,000, still the cost of 10,000 loaves. Of course, during that time you will probably have been paying off your loan, and eating some of the bread. But if you have not been able to for any reason, then the amount you owe should *feel* no bigger in 20 years' time than it does now. Of course, things are a lot better for Scottish students. Smug smiles north of the border.

Most ex-students want to get rid of their student loan. But be careful before you pay off more than you have to. There is no point in paying off your student loan if you then just borrow money more expensively on an overdraft or bank loan. Only pay extra amounts off your student loan if you are sure you won't have to borrow from the bank to survive at the end of the month. The easy lessons you learn as a student are the ones in the lectures and seminars. The hard – but just as important – ones are those taught to you by your bank.

> A friend of mine, now a financial journalist – if I mentioned her name you would say, 'Good grief! I'd never have believed that. Not of her!' – took out her first credit card when she went to university. Away from home, near to shops. We've all done it. How it worked, though, was a mystery to her. The credit card bill came and told her she had to pay a tiny amount. Far less than she had spent. An amount she could afford. She sent off a cheque. The card still worked, she could still buy stuff, so she spent more. The statements came each month and each month she paid a bit more. But she could manage it.
>
> You know where this is leading. I hope. It never occurred to her that she had to do more than pay the amount the card company asked. Soon she had a debt of half her student grant (this was some years ago, when students were given money, not debt). But she did not realize it. As long as she could afford the monthly bill, she still spent. Well-dressed, fun-loving, generous, she liked being a student. It was freedom. Why did people say managing your money was so difficult?
>
> Then the card stopped working. 'Rejected,' the shop said. Clothes back on the rack. She rang the customer service number she found on one of her statements (she kept them all in a box in the wardrobe). She had spent over her limit: £2000. The same as her grant. For a year. She had to work all summer, every summer, to pay it off. She knows how cards work now.

Banks are all too happy to offer students a current account, interest-free overdrafts and a credit card. They want you to get into the habit of banking – and debt – early. The important lesson to learn here is that if you treat your bank well, it will treat you reasonably well. But if you treat it badly, it will treat you appallingly.

There may be an incentive to open the account. NatWest, for example, currently offers a five-year railcard (which gives discounts on train tickets) worth £100, or £55 in cash. Banks will also offer interest-free overdrafts. Barclays, for example, gives you a £200 overdraft automatically, which you can extend to £1000, also interest-free, in the first year – if you ask – and £1500 interest-free in the third year. Again, if you ask.

Sounds good. But beware. If you go over the overdraft limit then *Zap!* You are charged interest at 27.5 per cent on the excess. If you don't have enough in your account to meet a payment you've made, then *Zap!* £30 is charged. And don't think writing your card number on the back of a cheque to guarantee it will help. If that cheque is honoured (because it was guaranteed by the number) but would otherwise have been returned, then *Zap!* £25 is taken off your money. And it's the same if you use your debit card to get cash or pay for stuff and it should have been returned unpaid but isn't. *Zap!* £25 taken off.

But, you say, you don't have any money. The bank is refusing to honour payments, so how can it *get* its £25? Well, that's the clever bit about banks. They control your bank account. So they just deduct the money and you are even more in debt.

Not that Barclays is unusual or the worst. It is, in fact, one of the best. These charges are normal. Or at least pass for normal in the world of banks. That's why the big five High Street banks in the UK made profits of more than £25 billion in 2003. Nothing wrong with profit. It's what the makes the world – or at least the commercial bit – go round. But your job is to make sure none of that is your money. Look at those profits again. More precisely they were £25,776,000,000. Those figures are rounded to the nearest £1 million. So they won't even notice if it's £25,775,999,975. But you will appreciate that £25. It's the price of a railcard for a year – and a sandwich at the station.

Write this on a Post-It note and keep it with your beer money:

DON'T MESS WITH YOUR BANK.
IT BITES BACK!

And the lessons don't stop when you graduate. At some point those comfy interest-free overdrafts will be turned into regular ones where interest is charged. And it's better to agree the overdraft than just ignore it. Otherwise you may get stung with those unauthorized overdraft fees.

All banks (except Co-operative) do pay some interest on your account. It is so small, at 0.1 per cent, it almost doesn't exist. For example, if you have a positive balance averaging £350 over the year then you will earn – wait for it – 35p interest. And you thought scientists invented nanotechnology! As a student the chances are you don't pay tax – the student loan and money from your parents is tax-free. Earnings and interest you earn on savings can be tax-free as long as you do not earn more than £4745 in the tax year (chance would be a fine thing!), so you should not be paying tax. But unless you tell the bank and register for tax-free interest you will have 20 per cent taken off it automatically and passed to the Inland Revenue. So instead of 35p you will get just 28p.

Ask the bank for form R85 and fill it in. Then the interest you earn – however derisory – is at least all yours. None of it – not even 7p – goes to the Chancellor! His pocket picked!

More seriously, make sure that any employer knows you are a student and check at the end of the year that you haven't paid tax you shouldn't have on your earnings. It is very common for people who are in and out of work to get taxed the wrong amount. If at the end of the tax year (5 April) your earnings are less than the personal allowance – currently £4745 – you should *not* have paid tax. And you can claim it back.

National Insurance contributions are more complicated. You have to pay those for any week when you earned at least £91. If you've earned less than that, you don't have to pay them, and your employer should not deduct them. Don't worry that you're not paying them. If you're a student there's no point in paying National Insurance contributions when you work in the holidays unless you pay enough during the tax year to make the year 'count' towards your pension (I know, I know, but that time will come round all too soon). And missing up to five years will not affect your pension, so it's probably not worth worrying about it just yet.

■ Buying a home

Property prices have never been so high in relation to earnings. The average pay for full-time employees is around £24,000. The average home costs around £160,000, more than six and half times as much. Most mortgage providers lend about 3.5 times your earnings. There's a big gap. How can you fill it?

Save up for a bigger deposit. If you save £76,000, you only need to borrow £84,000, which is 3.5 times your pay.

Earn more If you get promoted and earn £45,725, then you could borrow £160,000 at the standard 3.5 times. Nowadays, lenders recognize that many people earn bonuses and extra income so you are not confined to your main salary. If you have other regular items of income, you will find lenders who will take them into account.

Find a partner Many lenders will let you borrow 2.5 times your joint earnings. Some will go up to 2.75 times. So, if you are both on average pay (£24,000), you can borrow 2.75 x £48,000, which is £132,000, leaving only £28,000 to find for the deposit. Others say three times one income and one times the other, which is normally less. But if one of you earns more than three times what the other earns, it's better.

Go to a lender who will take account of what they call 'ability to pay' This is a new idea. The multiples-of-income method was devised a long time ago when interest rates were higher than they are now, and it does restrict people who have modest incomes but few other commitments. For example, if you wanted to borrow £160,000 and repay it over 25 years and your mortgage rate was 6.5 per cent, it would cost you £1080 a month. If you earned, say, £35,420 a year, you could only borrow up to £124,000 under the standard system of lending you a 'multiple' of your income. But if you *could* borrow £160,000 and took out a repayment mortgage at 6.5 per cent, the repayments would cost you exactly half your net income. That would be a struggle. But you might think it was worthwhile. If you were a couple, it would be even better. You would only need to earn £16,630 each to be able to repay the mortgage from half your net income.

Nowadays, some lenders recognize that many people can afford a mortgage even if the standard multiple of 3.5 times earnings indicate they cannot borrow enough. They will look at what you can afford, bearing in mind any other borrowing (and, yes, they do look at student loans). If your finances are not in too bad a state, you might be able to borrow four or even five times your salary. Which does make buying a home a bit more possible for many property virgins.

Borrow over a longer period The typical mortgage is over 25 years, but sometimes you can borrow for longer. It might be the only way to get your first foot on that long ladder called 'home ownership'. Why is it called a ladder? What's at the top? What if someone pulls it away? Is it unlucky to walk under it? No one knows.

Go 'interest-only' There are two types of mortgage. The first is a 'repayment mortgage': your monthly payment goes partly towards paying interest on the loan and partly towards repaying the capital. By the end of the 25 years, you will have paid off the loan in full and the property is yours. The other sort is an 'interest-only mortgage'. With this you only pay the interest on the loan. So you still owe the whole debt for the whole 25 years. So if you borrow, say, £160,000 to buy your home, 25 years later you will have paid interest on that for a quarter of a century but you will still owe £160,000. You may have to sell your home to repay it. But interest-only mortgages are a lot cheaper. £160,000 at 6.5 per cent interest-only will cost you just £866.67 a month, compared with £1080 for a repayment mortgage. But if you are so strapped for £213 a month that you can afford interest-only but cannot afford repayment, you are probably borrowing too much. And, of course, you still have to think about how you will repay the mortgage.

Find a good deal The standard rate for a mortgage is around 6.5 per cent a year, but you can do much better than that, at least for a short time. You can easily find rates about 1 per cent below this, which, on a 25-year mortgage, would save you about £100 a month. And you can find even better deals that last for, say, two years. Four per cent for two years, for example, will bring your repayment mortgage costs down to £844 a month. Even more affordable. In two years' time, you can look for a better deal. And by then, hopefully, you'll be earning more anyway.

Buy somewhere cheaper It might mean buying a home that is less nice, or smaller, or located somewhere less desirable. But it could be better than overstretching yourself.

There are hundreds of different mortgages. Literally. For example, if you wanted to borrow £144,000 on a £160,000 property, there are 511 different products to choose from. You can do your own research, or you can use a mortgage broker. But choose one you trust, which has a national reputation. Most brokers charge you a fee. A bit cheeky – because they also get paid by the company that lends you the money. But if you get the mortgage that is right for you, then it's money well spent.

There are lots of special deals about, offering, for example, a reduced rate or a fixed rate (for more on these see pages 139–44). The key thing with these is that you should be free to leave the deal and find another as soon as the special deal runs out. Some mortgage deals tie you in for longer than the deal itself lasts. Don't even think about them.

There is one unpleasant trick that some lenders play, mainly on first-time buyers, but it can apply to anyone who needs to borrow a very big proportion of the value of the property – it's known as 'loan to value', or LTV. Normally you will borrow 90 or 95 per cent and find the rest as a 'deposit'. So if your new home costs £150,000, you will have to stump up £15,000 or £7500 and then borrow the rest. If you are borrowing 90 per cent – or, indeed, more than 75 per cent with some companies – they will try to make you pay insurance called mortgage indemnity guarantee. That is normally abbreviated to 'MIG' because it sounds more friendly. But MIG is anything but friendly. It's another of these insurances where the person who pays the premium doesn't benefit. In other words, you pay for the lender to be insured if anything goes wrong!

You pay the premiums added on to your monthly payments. If you find you cannot afford to pay your mortgage, then the insurance protects not you but the lender. The lender will still eventually repossess your property and sell it at auction. But if that leaves the lender with a loss then the insurer will meet that loss. You get nothing. Except homelessness. Nowadays you can find loans without compulsory MIG. You should always try to do that.

Tax

When you do your sums, remember to take account of stamp duty land tax, or SDLT. If a property costs more than £60,000 you normally have to pay it. It's 1 per cent of the total price, rising to 3 per cent if the cost is more than £250,000, and a whopping 4 per cent if it's over £500,000. So on a £160,000 property it will be £1600. On a £260,000 property it will be £7800, and on a £560,000 property it will be – dramatic pause, roll of drums – £22,400. For nothing. Just bunce for the Chancellor.

There is one slim hope of avoiding it. If a property costs between £60,000 and £150,000, check its postcode on the Inland Revenue website. If it's in what's called a 'disadvantaged area', there is no SDLT to pay unless it costs more than £150,000.

And another even slimmer hope. If the price of the property is close to one of the limits, then it's well worth keeping the price below it. For example, a property that costs £250,000 is taxed at 1 per cent. But as soon is as the price goes higher, even £250,001, then the full tax of 3 per cent applies to the whole lot. So the tax goes up from £2500 to £7505 (the amount is always rounded up to the next fiver). Which is an extra £5005 tax on a £1 increase in the price. You could negotiate with the person selling the property to pay separately for any items they might be leaving behind, such as carpets or curtains. But things like fitted kitchens count as part of the house and cannot be sold separately.

Risks

Mass home-ownership is a relatively recent thing. Property prices have really only gone one way – up. However, many people remember the difficult times in the 1990s when prices fell. Between 1 April 1989 and 1 July 1995, a period of just over six years, they fell by 12.5 per cent – a loss that was reversed over the next two and a half years, when the average price rose to £70,560. Modest by today's standards.

Apart from those nearly nine years, house prices have risen relentlessly. But there is a danger that if you buy today at, say, £160,000, prices will fall and you could have paid too much.

Now that matters for two reasons.

If you have to sell If you do, you will lose money, getting back less than you paid. Losing £20,000 on the biggest deal of your life could leave you with a debt for a long time. But it only happens if you absolutely have to sell. If you can hang on, prices will almost certainly rise again.

There may be a rise in interest rates In 2003, rates fell to their lowest for 50 years and then started to rise slowly. If they doubled, could you still afford your mortgage? If not, you would have to sell and you could be faced with a big loss. That's what happened in the 1990s. Rates rose, people had overextended themselves, and they could not afford the repayments. So they were forced to sell. But their homes were now worth less than their loans. It was called negative equity. And it left thousands of people with no house but a big debt.

Negative equity could happen again. So if you buy, make sure you don't overextend yourself, however tempting it is to get the house of your dreams.

With prices rising and experts telling us that it 'can't go on for ever', people who are considering buying now have their own big question. Should I wait? The answer's no. Again, for two reasons.

First, no one knows whether or not house prices will fall. Every expert prediction about where house prices are going has been wrong. But then, experts usually are wrong about where markets are going. Buying before a rise or selling before a fall is called timing the market, and quite honestly no one can do it. Or if they can they live in an island paradise and keep the secret to themselves.

My two penn'orth, for what it's worth, is that prices will carry on rising. There's one iron law of economics: when something is in short supply, the price rises. And there is undoubtedly a shortage of housing. One reason for this is that we all expect more. We move out earlier. Between 1989 and 2000, the average size of a household fell from 2.9 people to 2.3. Every year there are 179,000 more households in England alone. One major factor in that is that more and more people are living alone. About one in three homes is now occupied by one person.

At the same time, we are building fewer homes. We have not built so few for more than half a century. In 1967–1968, when house-building peaked, we completed around 425,000 new homes. In 2002 it was just 134,000 homes. A government report estimates that at that rate, every home built today will have to last 1200 years. The current rate of building is about half what is needed in the long term to keep the rise in house prices down. There is no indication that this gap will be met in the near future. So house prices will continue to rise.

But whether they go up or not, a house is somewhere to live, not an investment – the second reason for buying now. The right time to buy a home is when you need it. If you need a home now, buy one now. And don't worry about what it's worth until you need to sell it.

■ Reaching fifty

Don't pretend you're sort of in your forties. There's no such thing as forty-ten. Still less forty-twelve. Once you have reached the half century, you have passed an important stage financially. Although you probably have 30 years of life left, there isn't that much time for long-term stuff. So play safe with your money once you have that big 5 at the start of your age.

Finance in your fifties can be very good or very bad. One thing is for sure, it will be different. Children leave home, retirement looms, debt recedes, some people inherit, others find an investment really does produce a lump sum. Others lose their job, perhaps for the first time in their life, and more and more divorce, with all the financial instability – never mind heartache – that can bring. And even if you are spared creeping infirmity, older relatives may not be and you can find yourself caring for them. So there are no rules. Apart, of course, from being sensible.

Pensions

These should be sorted out. First, the state pension. Contact the Department for Work and Pensions (DWP) and get a state retirement pension forecast – you can do it online or by phone. The basic pension (around £80 a week) is paid in full to most people, but many women, and those with a shortened work record, won't even get that. There is also an extra earnings-related pension. Sadly, this has been cut by successive governments, and although it can be as much as £140 a week, the average is more like £20. If your pension is less than you had hoped, see if you can pay extra contributions to boost it now.

Also, check for other pensions you may have paid into. It's very easy to lose track of old pensions but the money is there with your name on it and it's worth having, especially if you worked in the public service for even a few years. That can quite easily mean a four-figure pension. You can track down old pensions at the government-run Pension Schemes Registry.

If you're still working, it's not too late to join your company scheme. Or, if you are in it, to pay extra contributions to buy added years or to boost your pension pot with help from your employer.

If you see adverts for companies offering ways of taking money out of your pension early, ignore them. At least two have been stopped from trading and the Financial Services Authority has warned that for most people they all offer a very bad deal.

Work

If you are offered redundancy, think very carefully. It may reduce your pension, and any redundancy payment you get won't last that long. It's hard to get a new job in your fifties – age discrimination is rife. And would you – and your partner – be happy if you were at home all day?

More fashionable now is flexible retirement, phasing yourself out. From April 2006, you will be able to take your company pension, or some of it, and carry on working for the same employer. That can be a very good idea. But with life expectancy growing, you might just want to work on until you are 70, boosting the pension you will get and keeping yourself active and healthy.

Money

If you do get a lump sum – from redundancy, your pension, a distant aunt or an investment plan – don't rush into investing it. Keep it somewhere safe in a cash account earning interest for at least six months while you decide what to do with it. Think how much you want to spend in the long term and how much to treat yourself to in the short term. If you haven't got a cash ISA, put at least £3000 into one – remember a husband and wife can have one each – to keep at least the bit of interest it earns from the taxman. If you have debts, then paying them off – yes, even your mortgage – is probably the best thing to do with a lump sum. If you are going to have less income in the future, the last thing you need is interest payments draining your money.

Benefits

There may be money out there you can claim. Don't be afraid to ask for help from the state. But don't be disappointed when you see how little it is. Here are some of the benefits you might be able to claim.

- Jobseeker's allowance (if you are looking for work)
- Disability benefits (if you are ill or disabled)
- Income support (if you have a low income)
- Tax credits (if you are in low-paid work)
- Council tax discount (if you live alone)

To find out more, see Follow-up, pages 202, 203.

Home

If you have a home, the best way to turn it into cash is to sell it and move somewhere cheaper. At your age there is no other practical way of using its value. There will be expenses for lawyers, estate agents, surveyors, removers and, of course, decorators and builders when you move in to your new home. But if you are prepared to move to somewhere smaller or in another part of the country, there is definitely money to be made.

In this world, shipmates, sin that pays its way can travel freely, and without passport; whereas Virtue, if a pauper, is stopped at all frontiers.

Herman Melville

Chapter 5
Life's little difficulties

❏ Money in the bank

❏ Babies

❏ Sixth-formers

❏ Relationships

❏ Redundancy

Every life contains unforeseen events and times of difficulty. Jobs vanish, relationships end, dependants arrive. We move on. And we need to be prepared. How much do you have to meet an emergency? Everyone should have something. You need a new roof and the insurance won't pay up, the car blows up, your daughter is injured in Morocco and you have to fly out there, or, yes, you just want to run away for a few days – or for ever. It does happen. Some advisers say you should have at least three months' income stashed away. Some say six months' money. I'm not so sure. Although it sounds about right, I have said it before and I will say it again (and again until I'm blue in the face and you're no longer red in the bank account) – if you have a debt, pay it off before you save. That applies to emergency money too.

So emergency money does not always have to be cash. For example, if you are paying off the credit card, it is always possible to reverse that for a while and go back to borrowing. That's not as good as cash in the bank, but it's there as a sort of safety net to get you out of trouble for a short time.

Of course, if you don't deal with that debt, it will get you into more trouble later. And I know that people do like having some savings, even if they have a bit of debt. When I was first self-employed, I put a proportion of every cheque I was paid into a separate account to pay my tax when it came due. I also had a big overdraft facility with my bank. So if I had to go overdrawn I could do so without major penalties. Sometimes that meant I was overdrawn and had savings. I once worked out that over the year that way of doing things cost me about £40. It was the price of sleeping at night.

So it's up to you. Keep some money saved for those financial, domestic or emotional crises. Even if you have some debt. But please, please make sure it's earning a decent rate of interest. Or you can just make sure you have a bit of a credit line somewhere so that if the worst happens (let's hope not the worst, but something bad), at least you can use that facility to sort it out.

■ Babies

Aren't they great? Aren't they cute? Aren't they expensive! Having a baby can turn out to be the most expensive thing you ever do – and, of course, the best. But there are ways of reducing those costs.

Everything else we've looked at about spending wisely and so on applies equally to baby stuff. Don't feel you're being mean by being practical about what you need and how to afford it. But the other side of balancing the books is always getting more money in. And here the government does help.

Every parent is entitled to child benefit. And most of them claim it. Tax-free and paid every four weeks, it's £16.05 a week for the first child and £10.75 for each subsequent child. These rates go up every April. If you're a lone parent, you get £17.55 for the first child. That rate doesn't go up each April so in three or four years it will become the same as the standard rate for the first child. But if you are a single mum, it's well worth getting that extra.

Child benefit is normally paid to the mother. But if the mother works and the father is the one who stays at home to care for the child, then it's best to get it paid in his name. Because the person who gets the child benefit also gets help in qualifying for a state pension for the time they spend looking after the child.

Child benefit is paid by the Inland Revenue rather than the Department for Work and Pensions (DWP) – it's all part of Gordon Brown taking over things. And the Inland Revenue is responsible for the other help that people with children can get – child tax credit.

The child tax credit is a complex means-tested benefit. It is paid to anyone who has children, whether they work or not and whether they claim benefits themselves or not. So it's important for all parents to check what they are entitled to. The calculation is almost impossible. It is one of the most fiendish bits of arithmetic ever devised by the mathematical Torquemadas of the Inland Revenue. Week does not mean week, year does not mean year, amounts are rounded up, then rounded off. And the whole complex calculation is based on an income figure that is known to be wrong. So the money paid is always provisional and can be added to or taken away next year.

On top of that, if you want to claim childcare costs, then you have to claim something called working tax credit (WTC) as well. Oh, and neither of them has anything to do with tax, and they are not credits. They are benefits. Normally paid to the mother, into her bank account, though WTC can be paid to the mother or father through their pay packet. It might be designed to put people off. Perhaps it is. But don't let them win – make sure you get yours!

Child tax credit itself comes in three parts:

1. A family element of £545 a year, or £10.45 a week. Just about everyone gets this. You get the full amount if your income is up to
   £50,000 a year. That income is the joint income of both parents if
   they live together. If they don't, it's the income of the one who cares
   for the children. Above £50,000 the amount you get tapers off, and
   disappears altogether as the joint income reaches £58,818. So a
   couple in which each partner earns £29,500 would be considered too
   well off to get it.
2. A 'baby addition', added to the family element in the year the baby is
   born. This is another £545 or £10.50 a week. It tapers off as joint
   income reaches £58,818, and disappears as it hits £66,026.
3. A child element of up to £1445 a year or £27.71 a week for each
   child. This is seriously means-tested. It is paid in full where the income
   (joint again) is £13,480 a year or less. It is then tapered off as income
   rises and it disappears at an income of £17,879 for one child; add on
   £4400 for each other child to find the disappearing point.

To that we have to add WTC. This was intended to top up low or modest
incomes. But if you have children it can give a bit extra on top of quite a
decent wage. And if you pay for childcare, then as long as both caring parents are working you can get help up to very high incomes.

For example, if you have two children and pay the maximum amount for
childcare and you work full-time (and so does your partner, if you have one),
you can get some WTC if your annual income is up to £43,765. Again, add
on £4400 per child to find the limit for more children. You can work out what
you will get at the Inland Revenue website or by ringing their tax credit
helpline (see Follow-up, pages 202, 203).

Maternity, paternity
And don't forget, when you get pregnant, that you can get up to a year off
work. For the first six weeks you get 90 per cent of your pay. For the next 20
weeks you get statutory maternity pay, which in 2004–2005 is £102.80. For

the next six months you get no pay but you are entitled to have your job back at the end of your maternity leave. Of course, you may have an employer who gives you more generous maternity pay than that, but that's the minimum you should get. And dads are not forgotten – quite. They can have two weeks paternity leave and they get at least £102.80 a week for that. Or more if their employer is kind.

■ Sixth-formers

Babies grow up. And if you have children aged 16 to 19 at school, they might be able to get up to £30 a week during the term – and £100 bonus at the end of term – to help with the costs of staying on at school. These bonuses are called education maintenance allowances (EMAs) and they began only in September 2004 so it's very important that people claim if they think they're eligible. The EMA has to be paid direct into a bank account and it doesn't affect any other benefits, and is not taken away if the young person does part-time work. It's not taxable.

Not everyone can get the EMA. The income of their parents must be £30,000 a year or less, and to get the maximum it must be £19,630 a year or less. If there are two parents living together then their incomes are added together. The child will get between £10 and £30 for each week of term as long as they attend school regularly. And there will be up to five term bonuses of £100 if the young person meets agreed standards of behaviour and performance. Schools and colleges have the application forms. Call the EMA helpline and/or find out more about other financial help for 16- to 19-year-olds still at school or college (see Follow-up, Other benefits, page 203).

■ Money and love

First up. Do you get married? About three out of four married couples have cohabited before getting married. About two million unmarried couples live together – and many of them will never become husband and wife.

Leaving aside moral, religious or personal issues about marriage or cohabitation (which for the purposes of this book we'll ignore because they are too difficult), there is a very important legal difference. Married couples have a legal claim on each other's property – during marriage, after divorce and when one of them dies. Cohabiting couples don't. Or to sum up (it might be Post-It note time again):

WHAT RIGHTS DO MEMBERS
OF COUPLES HAVE?
MARRIED – TONS
UNMARRIED – NONE

There's no such thing as a common-law marriage. It doesn't matter how long you live together, or whether or not you have children. If you are not married, you have no rights. And that's it. But that's not what most people think. More than half of us think there *is* such a thing as a common-law marriage (abolished, in fact, in 1763!) and six out of ten of us think that couples who have lived together for a while have similar rights to married couples.

Now don't get me wrong. I'm not saying you should get married. But relationships are best entered into with your eyes open. If you see what I mean. Read on and all will be clear.

Property

A couple have lived together in a house for six years. They have both cared for the house, decorated it and cleaned it. But one of them owns it. The relationship ends. Does the non-owner have a right to stay in the property? Or to a share in its value?

What most people (57 per cent) think: yes.

The truth: no. It doesn't matter how much time or effort or even money the non-owning partner has put into making the home nice, without a legal document she (it usually is a she) can be thrown out with nothing.

If they are married: yes.

Money

A couple have lived together for two years. They seem deeply in love and do everything together. Both have a job – until one day, one of them loses their job and the other finds it very hard to manage financially. Does the working partner have an obligation to support the out-of-work partner?

What most people (55 per cent) think: yes.

The truth: no.

If they are married: yes.

Inheritance

A couple have lived together for ten years. Ditto decorating, etc. The richer partner dies without leaving a will. Does the surviving partner automatically inherit the deceased person's possessions – including their share of the home?

What about half of us (48 per cent) think: yes.

The truth: no. Without a will, brothers, sisters, parents, grandparents, cousins, aunts and uncles may all inherit some of their money. The unmarried partner gets nothing. And if there are no relatives? The estate goes to the government.

If they are married: the spouse gets most of it, but not necessarily all.

Inheritance tax

Ditto but there is a will and the money and the house are left to the partner. Is inheritance tax due?

What most people think: no data.

The truth: yes. If the estate is worth more than the limit, which was £263,000 in 2004–2005.

If they are married: no inheritance tax is due on anything left by a husband or wife to their spouse.

Children

If an unmarried couple has children – and 24 per cent of them do – who is responsible for the financial support of the children?

What most people (84 per cent) think: mother and father both have this responsibility.

The truth: mother and father both have this responsibility.

So the public got at least one right!

These survey results came from Advicenow, which is campaigning about living together and how to protect yourself if you're not married (see Follow-up, page 203).

Of course, same-sex couples – whether two men or two women – have no choice. They cannot get married. At the time of writing, plans to give them the right to sign a civil partnership agreement are on hold. If those plans go through, then same sex couples who sign the document would have just about the same rights as married couples. If they don't sign it, then they will be treated like unmarried opposite-sex couples. If the new law goes through, it will not give any new rights to opposite-sex couples. They will still have to get married to get the rights of married couples. It sort of makes sense.

Divorce

Things are much fairer – or at least much more equal, which may not seem the same thing – for a couple if they are married. Children complicate matters but most divorces now are on the 'clean break' principle. In other words, the ex-couple split their property and go their separate ways. Of course, on top of that there will be maintenance for the children and the person who cares for them. But the assets are split equally regardless of who brought what to the marriage or who earned most during it. And you can forget pre-nuptial agreements, whatever you saw in the film *Intolerable Cruelty*. They may work in the USA but they don't work in the UK. The courts here can take notice of an agreement signed by a couple before they marry, but it's not legally binding. So if you go into a marriage with much more property, money or earning power than your new spouse, be prepared to lose half of it if your marriage ends.

Splitting money and possessions is normally quite straightforward. But remember, three chairs are worth a lot less than half the value of six.

My father collected chess sets. One day he came home with a real treasure: a beautifully carved ivory set, which he bought for a bargain price. Except it wasn't a complete set. It was just the black pieces. The set had been split in an acrimonious divorce. So neither partner got the valuable asset. And Dad got a bargain.

Then we come to the hard stuff. Your home and your pension rights. The home will normally stay with the person who has care of the children. If neither of you does, then you can fight over it, sell it, or let one keep it and balance that against other assets. One partner may have the home, for example – and the mortgage – and the other the rest of the savings. It depends on what you have.

The right to a pension is very valuable, especially if either of you has built up rights to a public sector pension. The rights will have to be valued. That gives a figure called a cash equivalent transfer value, or CETV. This can be dealt with in three ways.

1. The value can simply be counted as part of the assets to be split. One party may keep the whole of the pension as long as the other gets something worth as much. If the CETV is £100,000 and the marital home is also valued at £100,000, one partner could have the house and the other the pension. It's called 'offsetting'. But usually it's not so easy.

2. It can be 'earmarked' so the pension stays where it is but each can draw on it when they reach pension age. This is not very common.

3. It can be split. For example, if one of you is a teacher and has the right to a pension worth £25,000 a year, index-linked, then the CETV might be around £500,000, and the pension fund would have to transfer half that sum to a pension in the other spouse's name. Pension-splitting remains rare, and is not suitable for pensions that are not very valuable.

It's important to get a good solicitor – not to screw your ex for every penny you can but to make sure a sensible and fair settlement is reached. You can find lawyers who specialize in amicable and efficient divorces through the Solicitors Family Law Association (see Follow-up, Couples, page 203).

Just because you've got half the stuff, don't think you will be as well off. Two can live as cheaply as one – together. But two people living separately will need two washing machines, two televisions and maybe two cars. So divorce will leave you poorer. Financially, as well as in other ways.

■ Relationships

Although it's called 'relationships', this section isn't about sex. It's about living together. And sharing. Money. How do you do it? Some people really throw themselves into relationships. They think because they share a bed they have to share everything – car, house, holidays, bank accounts. But I'm going to show you now that you don't. At least when it comes to bank accounts.

I've just made it up but it sounds like an old proverb: 'Sex starts relationships, money ends them.' Old cynic I may be, but Relate, the charity that helps couples with relationship difficulties, says that money is the biggest source of arguments. Not sex. Not selfishness. Not complete and utter disregard for *my* feelings, you bastard. But money. And anyone who has experienced coupledom will know that arguments about spending, borrowing, earning, saving and sharing money can ruin a perfectly lovely evening.

Now this is not a book about how to have a successful relationship – except, of course, that lifelong union between you and your money! My friends, family and loved ones might smirk when they hear I'm writing a book about money. But they would fall about laughing and demand compensation if I told them I was writing about relationships! So I'm not. But when people live together – and that includes children and housemates as well as spouses and lovers – they do share stuff, sometimes even their income. And they can cost each other money.

Nowadays, most couples start by living together before they get married. The last section talked about relationships ending. Here we look at the exciting stuff. Getting together, moving in, sharing a home. And joint bank accounts. Aaarrgghhhh! Also known as recipes for disaster. Even if you are married, and legally what's his is hers and what's hers is his, having a bit of your own money is as important as having your own bit of space.

Joint accounts are a strange thing. You both own the money. And you are both liable for any debt. The bank will pursue the easier target – whichever of you has the most money, or the money that's easiest to get at.

Scenario 1 You have a joint bank account and both your salaries go into it. Your partner is much worse about money than you. He goes overdrawn, without asking the bank, and whammy there's a £30 charge on the account and at some point some interest is charged. Who pays it? Well, you both do. Because it's a joint account. Not fair, is it?

Scenario 2 You inherit £5000. You pay the cheque into your joint bank account. Who owns it? You both do. He is free to write a cheque for £5000 for that second-hand Harley Davidson he has drooled over, rust and all. All you can do is shout. Or sulk. And it doesn't matter if you're married or not.

Scenario 3 You get so completely fed up with him that you decide to leave. One problem has been that the bank account is always overdrawn and now you owe the bank £2500 and interest is ticking up on it. He is out of work and cannot pay. You have a job. The bank comes after you for the money. Even though he did the spending. You decide to cut your losses and offer half, thinking that's more than fair. The bank says, 'No. You are liable for all of it because he cannot pay.' If you don't pay they threaten court action. All you can do is pay up. And no point in sulking. You've already left him!

So let's do this another way. You open a bank account with your salary. You operate it over the internet, never go overdrawn and earn interest on it. He opens one with his. Well, actually, he already has one at his local High Street bank. He is often overdrawn, often pays bank charges and is in a bit of a mess. You both open a joint account for genuine joint expenses. You work out that you have to put in £150 a month each to pay for gas, electricity, telephone, water and council tax. And you have to share the £500 a month for the rent. So that's £400 each a month. Then all those bills are paid by standing order or direct debit from that account. Of course, it can still all go wrong. If his money is such a mess that his direct debit does not go in, then that can be difficult. But it does mean that once you've paid that £400 a month, all the rest of your money is yours. In your own account. And you can spend it as you want. Without him complaining, or even knowing.

Groceries you can take in turns. Or if you are really organized, put in another say £150 a month each and pay those from the joint account too. It helps stop arguments about money. You have your own money for your own stuff, and you have joint money for your joint expenses.

If you can set that up, then you have at least started talking about money. And there is one thing that may crop up in those discussions. Who earns the most? In most couples one person does earn more. And if it's significantly more, that raises a *difficult question*. If you earn different amounts, do you contribute to the joint expenses 50–50? Or in proportion to your earnings? Suppose you earn £20,000 and your lover earns £40,000. And your joint expenses come to £450. It's obviously much harder for you to find £225 a month out of your £1268 net take-home pay than it is for him out of his £2357. So you might think that you should pay £150 and he should pay £300. On the other hand, if you do use half the electricity, half the gas, half the telephone (and no arguments here, please, about who natters on to their mum for hours) and eat half the food, why shouldn't you pay for it?

There is no easy answer to this. Different couples – among those who have even thought about it – come to different answers. One answer might be to pay for half of all those things and then let him treat you when it comes to choosing a more expensive holiday. Or paying for meals out. But the important thing is to talk about it. Because in one way money *is* like sex. And I don't mean you always want more and it never lasts long enough! What I mean is that if you talk to each other about it, there will be fewer misunderstandings. Things will be less likely to go wrong – and end your relationship.

When poverty comes in at the door, love flies out the window.

Anon

Discussing money is hard enough when things are going well. When they go badly, it's much more difficult. Each blames the other for the debts, the lack of income, or just being so unfair. So talk before things get bad. Sort finances out early and things will be easier if difficulties arise later.

And one final word on deception. It is very common in couples for one or both members to lie about the cost of something they've bought for themselves, or even to hide an expensive item so their partner does not notice. But lying and deceit about spending can be as bad for the relationship as lying about other things – especially if you are found out. You might be thinking of sex. I couldn't possibly comment!

■ Equality

Men and women are not equal. No! Stop! Put that down a minute and listen. Look at the facts. Women earn less than men. Women are more likely to work part-time than men. Women pay less into their pension. And when they draw it they will get less because they live longer and the money has to stretch further. It has to stretch further in adult life too. Women are the ones who bear the children and that means times of greater dependence – usually on men. Careers are interrupted, income falls, savings are spent. So even women who earn salaries as high as men's when they work are unlikely to earn as much altogether over the 40 or 50 years of their working lives. As a result, women generally own less than men. So economically women are definitely not equal.

That means that when it comes to money, as in so many other things, women have to try harder and work harder just to have a hope of equality. One way that women do try harder is paying into a pension. Over the last 20 years the proportion of men paying into a pension at work has been falling – from 66 per cent to 54 per cent. But among women who work full-time, the proportion has grown slightly over the same period – from 55 per cent to 58 per cent. And among women who work part-time, the growth has been even greater, helped by changes in the law that give part-timers equal rights to join a pension scheme. There the proportion has grown from 13 per cent to 31 per cent. But more needs to be done. It's even more true for women than for men that if their employer has a pension scheme they should join it. The employer will pay in too. So if they don't join, they're turning down a pay rise.

Now, I am a man. So just allow me three sentences to put the man's point of view. Because men don't necessarily feel that they have it easy economically. Not at all. The other side of the inequality is that men – or at least fathers – spend a lot of their lives earning money to keep other people. Part of that is a hangover from decades ago when married women were not even allowed to work (in the civil service women were dismissed on marriage, and many women who worked in banks were expected to leave, or at least to leave the pension scheme, on their wedding day). So a man was expected to keep his wife and children. And partly it is the biological fact that women bear children and that creates sometimes lengthy periods in their lives when they are dependent. Sometimes on the state. But very often on men. And many men – bless them – do see their role as earning the money to keep women and children in those times. OK, eight sentences.

So it's important that men and women both think about their own financial needs – and those of their partner. How do *they* feel about being dependent? Or earning the most? What do *they* feel they've given up for this relationship? Freedom? A job? Independence? Make sure it's worthwhile.

■ Redundancy

Losing your job is a shock at any time. But it's important to be practical. Fight for what you can get. But don't become obsessed with the unfairness of it. Take what compensation you can and move on. Getting a new job is more important than vengeance for losing the last one.

If you are made redundant you are being dismissed and you have rights. If you have worked for your employer for at least two years you have the right to redundancy pay. It's not much. A week's pay for each year of service aged 22 to 40 and 1.5 week's pay for each year worked from 41 to 64. There is an upper limit on what a week's pay is – £270 from February 2004. So you cannot get more than £8100 in redundancy pay. If your employer has gone bust or does not pay you, you can get help – and eventually the money – from the government's Insolvency Service Redundancy Payments Office (see Follow-up, page 204).

However, many employers will give you more. Indeed it may be in your contract. A month's pay for each year's service is normally the maximum and redundancy money up to £30,000 is tax-free. But make sure the redundancy process was done properly or the Inland Revenue may try to tax you on it. In particular, you must be sent a letter saying you have been dismissed and the reason given must be that your job is redundant.

Now, £30,000 may seem a lot of money. But it will soon go and the most important thing to do with it is put it into a safe, high-interest account, spend it as slowly as possible and find another job.

Of course, the news that you are to be made redundant might be as welcome as a thistle patch on a nudist beach. In that case, you should consider challenging your dismissal. If the redundancy process was not done properly you might be able to claim unfair dismissal. In particular, the selection of people for redundancy must have been done fairly. And you must normally be offered another job within the company if there is one.

■ Financial exclusion

> Like dear St Francis of Assisi I am wedded to poverty, but in my case
> the marriage is not a success.
>
> *Oscar Wilde 1854–1900*

Around two million adults do not have any sort of bank account. And around three million do not have a current account. Some people have just never had one. Others have got into financial difficulty and given them up, or found that their bank has closed the account and other banks have refused to take them on. That can cause great difficulties. Because nowadays just about everyone needs a bank account. State benefits and tax credits are paid into a bank account rather than in cash at the post office. And most employers prefer to pay that way too. Many financial deals are not available to people without a bank account.

In the past the banks were not that interested in opening accounts for people on limited incomes or with bad credit records, but now they all have a range of what are called basic bank accounts, which are especially designed for people in these circumstances. Basic bank accounts are current accounts except that normally they don't have a chequebook or a debit card – you withdraw cash using a cash card. They also don't allow overdrafts. Nor do they pay interest on the credit balance. Basic bank accounts are normally operated through the person's local branch, but most have telephone or even internet access. With some banks money that is paid in usually takes six working days rather than three or four to clear. But if you have got into financial difficulties and want to start again, a basic bank account can be a good way to go.

If you can count your money, you don't have a billion dollars.

John Paul Getty

Chapter 6
Debt and borrowing

❑ Good and bad ways of borrowing

❑ The difference between borrowing and debt

❑ The credit crunch

❑ How to control your debt

❑ Bankruptcy

Debt is growing. It is part of our way of life. But there is good and bad borrowing; sensible debts and stupid ones. Borrowing isn't always the same as debt. Here we sort out the good from the bad and the downright ugly.

In June 2004 the UK population crossed what broadcasters love to call a 'psychologically important barrier'. By which they mean a big round number was reached. And in 2004 our total debt reached a very big round number. The biggest round number most of us will ever come across. In June 2004 the total debt of adults in the UK reached a trillion pounds. A trillion is big, very big. It's a million times a million. So if you cannot imagine even a million pounds, it's a million times bigger than that. It is a 1 with 12 noughts after it – £1,000,000,000,000. In fact, the total debt was a bit more than that – it was £1,004,290,000,000. To the nearest million.

Given that most of this money is owed to a small number of banks and they charge us anything from 5 per cent to 30 per cent a year on it, we are paying back at least £50 billion a year in interest on debt. That doesn't buy us anything or get us stuff. We pay it to borrow what we spend. Frightening.

■ Big numbers

Any book about money contains big numbers. Millions, billions, even trillions. What do they mean? Human beings are good at small numbers. Throw a few coins on the table. If there are less than about seven, you can tell how many there are without counting them. Above seven, we have to count. So we are not very good at imagining big numbers. We normally do it by splitting things into groups. If there are two groups of five we can spot those as ten without actually counting, but if there are ten random coins we cannot say how many there are. People have ten fingers and this may be why our arithmetic goes up in tens. But as human beings we cannot even recognize the number of things in this most basic group without counting them. Ten groups of ten is 100 and ten times that is 1000. It is hard to imagine even 1000 things. And 1000 is quite a small number. Nowadays most people in the UK in full-time work get at least £1000 each month in pay. (If you take home £1000 a month, then your gross pay, before tax and National Insurance contributions, is £15,195 a year, or £293 a week.) So if we think of 1000, then a million is

1000 times 1000. That is your £1000-a-month pay a thousand times. Or as much as you would earn in 83 years: about two working lifetimes. Above a million they go up in thousands again. A billion is a thousand times a million. We've got used to a billion. Marks & Spencer was valued at £10 billion recently. Above that we get into the realms of the really big companies. Britain's biggest company, BP, is worth almost £100 billion. But we need ten BPs to go up again to a trillion. In fact, what we owe as a nation is enough to buy just about every company in the UK. It's the total amount that every company and everyone working in the UK produces in a year.

A trillion pounds. Suppose the total debt of Britain was put into £10 notes and a bank teller was set to counting them. Tellers accurately count around five notes a second, and human beings live for around two and a half billion seconds. So from birth to death, without breaks, she could count only around £125 billion pounds. One-eighth of the total amount we owe. If you were to make this exercise a smidge more realistic and base it on real working weeks in real working lives, you'd need 77 tellers to count a trillion pounds – assuming they did nothing else every working day for 40 years.

So it is a lot of money. But should we be worried? Not necessarily. Most people cope with their debt. And debt, within reason, is not a bad thing. It's the way the world works now. Even the government says that consumer credit is central to the UK economy. In other words, we all need to borrow to buy the stuff we need – or want. There are very few people today who have not borrowed money at some point in their lives. And that doesn't matter. Because as with most things in life, there is good debt and bad debt. There is even positively evil debt. But we will come to the Night of the Evil Debt later.

Most of the trillion pounds we owe is, in fact, good debt. The very best debt is the money we borrow to buy our home. A mortgage is not like other debt. That is because the money we owe is never more than the value of the home we buy. (In fact, if you've been paying attention, you'll know it's not quite 'never', more like 'hardly ever'. See Risks, page 85, for a discussion of negative equity.) In other words, although we have a socking great debt – the biggest most of us will ever see – we also have an asset that is worth even more. And one which normally goes up in value, while the debt stays the same or gets less. If worst comes to worst, you can sell the asset to pay the debt. Try doing that with clothes or a television you've bought on credit!

The latest estimate is that the value of all the homes in the UK is around £3 trillion. Whereas the total amount owed on them is around £827 billion. So as a nation we own far more than we owe.

Although it is ideal to have no debt, if you must borrow, then a mortgage is the best debt to have. Apart from anything else, the charge that is made for the loan is also one of the cheapest debts you will ever have. You could do a little test here and write down two sorts of debt that are cheaper than a mortgage. Answers at the end of this chapter.

There is another thing about borrowing for your home. Although you normally borrow the money over 25 years, the home you buy will almost certainly last a lot longer – a hundred years or more. And that meets the Golden Rule of Borrowing. Which is this:

■ GOLDEN RULE OF BORROWING

- ■ Never borrow to buy something that will last less time than the debt

For example, money you borrow to pay for Christmas should not be hanging around when the festive season comes back next year. Because then you will have to borrow for the next Christmas while you are still paying for the last one. Same with holidays. If you take two holidays a year, never borrow to pay for either of them over more than six months each. And if you buy those dream shoes you only wear twice, make sure you have paid off that bit of your credit card by the last time you wear them.

Short-term debt is about bringing spending forward a few weeks or months, maybe as long as a year. Credit cards are the best way to do that, if you are careful (more on this later). Short-term debt can be good debt, as long as it does not get out of hand.

Borrowing for bigger items, such as a washing machine or a car, is also part of what most of us have to do. It's hard to find a few hundred pounds – even harder to produce a few thousand – for something that you just have to buy. So you borrow it. Again, make sure you will repay the money before the item wears out. So borrowing for a washing machine for a couple of years is good, but if it's a major TV surround-sound system and you think you can only afford it if you buy it over five years or more, then you should pick something cheaper. These kinds of debt can spread the cost of something you need over a manageable period – say two to five years max – but if you have to spread repayments further than the item will last, then it means that you couldn't afford it in the first place. There's more on how to make sure this kind of borrowing costs you as little as possible later.

Finally there are those b i g items – the fitted kitchen, the smart bathroom, the decking. These are really home owners' items. (If you don't have a home, you shouldn't borrow over more than about five years.) If you *are* a home owner, and you are tempted to buy these things, you may also be tempted to cut the cost by securing the debt on your home. In other words, if you don't keep up the payments on the debt, then the bank can repossess your home. You should avoid that if you can. But, if you have to, securing debts like these on your home is an acceptable way to make long-term improvements to it. (Decking?!) But if you want to extend your home, make sure you don't overextend your borrowing. Don't put your home at risk for a wooden platform in your back garden.

Another way of looking at good debt and bad debt is that you control good debt. With bad debt, it controls you.

Here are the many ways you can borrow – in order of goodness!

■ From yourself

'Neither a borrower nor a lender be.' That is the advice given in *Hamlet* by Polonius to his son Laertes before he sets off on his travels. Nowadays, of course, we are all both. We borrow to buy our home, our car, our kitchen, our holidays and our shopping, paying out billions of pounds in interest every year. But at the same time we are encouraged to lend, or as the banks call it, save. We are supposed to save money for our retirement in a pension fund, save money for our kids in a child trust fund, or save for ourselves in an individual savings account.

The government encourages us to save by offering tax relief of one sort or another. And an army of 148,000 financial advisers persuades us it is a good idea. In fact, more than an army. The British Army only consists of 102,000 soldiers.

But look at the arithmetic. We use our credit card to do the shopping and never quite pay it off. So over the year we owe an average of £1000 on that. Suppose the interest rate is 15.9 per cent. We pay the bank £159 over the year to keep that debt going. On the other hand, we are encouraged to save – which is in effect lending money *to* the bank. The bank pays us, nowadays, 4 or 5 per cent at the most, so if we save £1000 in a savings account we earn £40. And usually we will pay tax on that, leaving us with £31.20. So the net cost of borrowing £1000 and saving £1000 over the year is the £159 it costs minus the £31.20 we make, which is a loss of £127.80. Instead it is much better to use any money you have available to pay off your debt. Do that first before you start saving. If you used the £1000 to repay the debt instead of borrowing on credit , you would be £159 better off over the year. It might even pay for a couple of Christmas presents.

So the first place to borrow money is – from yourself. It is the cheapest debt on the market. And if you cannot make a repayment, you're not likely to send the bailiffs round!

■ Credit cards

I like credit cards. A brilliant invention of the 1960s, they have transformed the way we live. But it's only in the last ten years that competition has driven down the cost. So much so, that borrowing on a credit card can now be the cheapest way to borrow – if you are careful.

The first time a card was used to pay was in New York in February 1950. Frank McNamara founded the Diners' Club and invented the card as an easy way to pay without cash. It was first used when he and business partner Ralph Schneider had dinner in Major's Cabin Grill. Bankers still reverently call the event The First Supper. At the start, 200 Diners' Club members could use the card in 27 smart New York restaurants. But within a year, 20,000 people had signed up, as had hundreds of retailers. Within two years it was accepted in thousands of shops and eateries and had spread to other countries. Diners' Club, and American Express which followed in 1958, were charge cards – the debt had to be paid off in full each month. A year later in 1959 the Bank of America in California issued the first true credit card, where the debt could be rolled over and interest was charged. The Bankamericard spread to other states in 1966. And in the same year Barclays Bank established Barclaycard in the UK. The modern world had begun.

The basics: You buy stuff. You pay with the card. The bank pays the shop, keeping about 25p for every £10 spent. At the end of the month the bank sends you a bill for what you have bought. You can pay it off in full and there is no charge. You can pay some of it off, as little as £5 in some cases, and you owe the rest to the bank. It adds on interest. So you owe the bank for what you have bought and the interest. But the banks have taken a simple idea and made it a complicated game. And as they make the rules – and decide the penalties – it can be very expensive to play.

First, there are the penalties:

■ You miss the payment date, even by one day – a fine of up to £25.

■ You spend more than the limit on your card – another fine of up to £25.

Second, there are the extra charges:

■ You use the card abroad – £2.75 for every £100 you spend.

■ You draw out cash – £2 each time and more if you draw out more than £100.

■ You draw out cash – the interest rate is higher and starts being charged at once.

Third, there are the cunning plans. Credit card companies will often send you a 'credit card cheque' through the post. It may even be made out to you for a certain amount. But if you pay it into your bank account you will have to pay:

■ £2 for every £100 on the cheque. So £40 if it is for £2000.

■ A higher rate of interest and it starts at once.

Fourth, they charge high rates of interest. Borrowing money over a long period on a credit card is expensive. Typical interest rates are around 16 per cent. In other words, if you borrow £1000 over a year you will pay £160 in interest. But you can borrow it and pay nothing! Credit card companies want our business, so they offer special deals – and some of them are very good.

The advice you read about credit cards – including the advice here – assumes you have a good credit rating and that you can pick and choose which card you use. That is not true for everyone. If you have been refused credit, read the next pages. But read carefully The credit crunch on page 127.

Free credit

Although credit cards normally charge high rates of interest, they also offer to charge you nothing – zero per cent. There are two kinds of zero per cent card: the balance transfer card and the spending card, plus some cards that offer a combination of the two.

Zero per cent balance transfer You can move a debt from another card or cards and pay no interest on it. Yes, of course there is a catch. The offer only lasts a fixed time. Usually six months, but you can now get nine- or even twelve-month offers. For that time your debt is free. If you have a debt at a high rate with another credit card company – or even a bank, some will let you transfer overdrafts and other debts – these cards are a great idea. Move your debt, divide it by six (or nine or twelve) and pay it off over the free period. Never keep the debt there longer than the zero per cent offer lasts. At the end of the free period, the balance will be charged at a much higher rate.

If your debt is too big to pay off in that time, you have two choices. Pay as much of it as you can while the zero per cent lasts and then move it to another zero per cent card. Or move the debt at the start to a card with a low 'life of balance' transfer rate. These do not offer zero per cent. But they can offer a very low rate on your transferred debt. See Paying off debt, page 136.

So how do they do make money? If they normally have to charge 16 per cent, how can they afford to charge new customers zero per cent? First, they lose money on these deals. They hope you will move your debt and stay with them, paying a higher rate later. Second, some charge you a higher rate for your spending. If you also use the card to buy stuff, your monthly payment goes to pay off your debt. Any new spending is charged at a high rate. And you cannot pay it off until you have cleared the debt completely. So the rule is to move your debt and never use the card for spending. Cut it up.

Moving your debt from one zero per cent card to another can mean free credit for a very long time. Welcome to the world of the rate tart. Someone who moves their account often just to get absolutely the best rate. If you are well organized, and happy to do your finances regularly and move money on a precise day, then rate tarting can save you money.

Rate tarting is not just for those with debts they want to move. Suppose you have a debt on a credit card and you earn or come into some money – enough to pay it off. The best advice is normally to use your money to pay off your debt. But if you move your debt to a zero per cent card, and invest the money at say 4 per cent, you are earning interest on your money and paying none on your debt. Quids in! But beware the traps. You have to do your accounts on the right day or risk ending up losing a lot of what you've made. Tarts have to know precisely where to be, and when, to get the best return!

Zero per cent spending card Some cards will offer you zero per cent interest on everything you spend. Again, it's usually for a fixed period of six to twelve months. These cards are very good value for doing the Christmas shopping or spreading the cost of a big item over a few months. But beware. At the end of the free period, interest rates whack up. And remember, this is not free money. The debt does have to be paid off, even though you are not being charged any interest. So don't go mad with the card!

A combination of the two Nowadays, there are some cards that offer zero per cent on transferred balances and zero per cent on spending too. The best of both worlds. But also the best of both temptations. At the end of the interest-free period you can find yourself with a frightening debt. So take extra care with these.

Cheap borrowing

If you play it carefully, you can sometimes use cards for cheap borrowing.

Balance transfer card If you have a big debt that is hard to manage, you should take out a new card that lets you transfer your balance and then pay it off at a very low interest rate until it is cleared. It doesn't matter if you take a year or ten years, the deal lasts for the 'life of balance'. At the moment the best deal is charging just 3.9 per cent on the debt. Once you get the card, cut it up as soon as the debt is transferred.

A good permanent low rate Many people do not want to spend their time worrying about the best credit card deal and finding the best rate and moving money around. So if you are in the habit of using your card to buy things, and you let some of the debt ride over from time to time, then get a card with a good, permanent low rate. These are generally cards that you operate over the internet. The best rate at the time of writing is 5.9 per cent, which is exceptional and may not last. Never pick a spending card that charges more than 10 per cent. And never let the debt remain for a long time. If it does, you are spending more than your income. And that is always bad news.

Cheap spending

Some cards offer 'cheap spending' deals and rewards. But beware. They may not be as good as they seem.

Cashback or money off Every time you use your credit card, the bank charges the retailer for the service. Normally, it's about £2.50 for every £100 you spend. So if you spend £100, the shop keeps £97.50 and sends £2.50 to the bank. Some cards give some of that money back to you. It's like a price cut on everything you buy. But don't get too excited. The amounts involved are small. With almost all the deals, you get just 50p back for every £100 you spend. So if you spend £120 a month on your card, you will get £7.20 back at the end of the year. Cashback is only worthwhile if you clear your debt in full without fail every single month. Interest on even a modest debt will wipe out a whole year's cashback in a month. For example, suppose you leave £600 owing on your card for one month. On a typical card with 15.9 per cent interest you will be charged £7.44 interest that month, which is more than the £7.20 cashback you got in the year.

Normally I criticize the financial services industry for using obscure and meaningless words. But cashback is different. It is a simple term. The trouble is it's used for two completely separate things. First, when you pay at the supermarket with your credit card they will always ask, 'Do you want cashback?' In other words, while you're paying shall we take a bit more out of your bank account and give it you as cash? It means the supermarket has less cash to handle. Second, it is used for cash rewards. Every £100 you spend, you get given 50p back by the bank. That's what we're talking about here.

Other rewards Other rewards are not worth having. Some cards give air miles or vouchers or points. But the amounts are tiny and there's also the hassle factor of saving them up and using them. On average they are worth 0.5 per cent of what you spend or less. So you're better off with cashback – it's money you can spend as you like. Some cards give money to charity. They're a waste of time too. They typically give 0.25 per cent of what you spend to the charity. So if you spent £120 a month on the card, the charity would get just £3.60 a year. If you want to give to charity, why not take out a cashback card and make an annual standing order for the amount you save through gift aid (see page 64). If you spend £120 a month on the card, you could give £7.20 at the end of the year and gift aid would boost that to £9.23. A much better deal all round.

Don't get stung!

However wisely you play your cards, the advantages can be wiped out by a moment's carelessness. Miss a payment or go over your spending limit and you will be hit with a penalty charge. These range from £10 to £25, and some banks will charge you each month until the problem is resolved.

▚ THE GOLDEN RULE OF CREDIT CARDS

Set up a direct debit to make at least the minimum monthly payment

That way you know it's paid each month and you won't be hit with an extra £25. You should also keep an eye on your credit limit. Going over it can cost you £25, so never use your card unless you are sure that it will not take you over the limit. Here's a typical scenario: your limit is £2000. You have had a series of expenses and your debt on the card is £1960, which you intend to pay off over the next year. You meet some friends and go out for a meal. Short of cash, you pay with your card and they give you their share in cash.

For the three of you the meal is £60. They give you £40 in cash but you go over your limit and the credit card company charges you £25. And you end up paying interest on the lot. It's the most you've ever paid to get your hands on four tenners! Except those tickets to hear Carreras, Domingo, Pavarotti, and ... hmmm, was there ever a fourth?

Here are some other things to watch out for.

Minimum payment The amount you have to pay each month is known as the minimum payment. It's not very much – some cards will accept as little as 2 per cent of what you owe. Suppose the card charges you 17.9 per cent a year and only expects you to pay 2 per cent of the debt each month. If you start with £1000 and make the minimum payment, how long will it take you to clear? The answer is 25 years! And over that time you will have paid £1800 in interest. If the company demands a bit more, say, 3 per cent a month repayments, then you clear the debt in half the time and pay £670 in interest. If you pay 5 per cent a month, then the debt disappears in seven years and you pay £361 in interest. So even if your card company only demands 2 per cent, always pay more. The card companies will guide you to make one of two choices: you can clear the debt every month, or pay the minimum. There is a third option. You can pay a fixed amount each month. But that's not always what you want. If you cannot afford to pay the whole lot off at once, the best thing to do is to pay the minimum by standing order – to avoid those late-payment fines – and then each month write a cheque, or pay online, to pay as much as you can afford off what you owe.

Cash Your credit card is for borrowing. It is *not* a cash card. Every time you take cash from a cash machine with a credit card you will be charged at least £2. In other words, you take out £20 and the machine gives you £18! Of course, it doesn't do it like that – it would be too obvious. It gives you £20 but then adds £2 to what you owe. So for £20 you are paying £22. You will also start paying interest on the cash – and the £2. Credit card companies charge you a higher rate of interest on cash than anything else. And the interest is charged at once and added on daily. So even if you pay your bill off each month in full, you will pay some interest on the cash. Indeed, one company, Capital One, thought up an even better ruse – the way its billing worked, you could end up paying interest for ever on cash you'd taken out!

Despite these penalties, in 2003 we drew £6.6 billion a year out of cash machines using a credit card. That means we probably paid the banks around £200 million a year in fees alone, apart from the extra interest. We made a present to the banks of around £4 million every week – for doing nothing.

The temptation to use your credit card as a cash card will grow as the new chip & PIN cards come in. At the moment few people even know the PIN for their credit cards. But in future we all will, because we'll have to use it instead of signing when we buy things. And that will enable us to pop our credit card into the cash machine as easily as our debit card. A big mistake.

There is one occasion when drawing out cash on your credit card is the lesser of two evils. If you have no money in your bank account and cannot use your debit card – or you would incur hefty overdraft charges if you did – then it *might* be cheaper to use your credit card. But do remember the cost and do pay off the cash debt as soon as you can. And if you are in this position, it really is time to sort out your finances.

Spending abroad If you use your credit (or debit) card abroad, you will normally be charged £2.75 for every £100 you spend. What for? No one knows. It is just what the banks do. It is called foreign currency loading and it is like a tax on using your card outside the UK. Only Nationwide cards do not make this charge anywhere in the world, though a couple of others have no loading in Europe. If you do a lot of shopping abroad – or in foreign currency on the internet – get a Nationwide card and pay it off in full each month.

If you draw out cash abroad with your credit card you will pay the foreign currency loading *and* the £2 minimum charge for taking out cash. So it's an expensive way to get cash when you are outside the UK. Better to use a debit card than a credit card.

Store cards Most big shops will offer you a store card. You can use it to buy goods in that shop, and sometimes in other stores belonging to the same company. Don't be fooled by the name. A store card is a credit card. If you do not pay off the amount you owe in full each month, you will be stung with interest of about 30 per cent. In other words, if you keep a debt of £100 on it all year you will be charged £30 in interest. For nothing. If you have store cards, pay them off and cut them up. Use a credit card. They are cheaper and more flexible. One thing: many people are tempted into getting a store card by the offer of 5 per cent or 10 per cent off what they are buying when they first take it out. This is a good deal! Take out the card, get the discount, cut the card up and pay it off in full when you get the bill. Quids in.

How to use credit cards wisely

- If you use it regularly but pay off the balance in full every month:

  Go for a card that offers cashback.

- If you use it regularly, usually pay off the balance, but sometimes, such as Christmas, let a debt run on:

  Go for a card with a permanent low interest rate.

- If you use it regularly, but seldom or never pay it off in full:

  Get two new cards: a zero per cent spending card, which will save you money, and a balance transfer card for the rest.

- If you have a manageable debt to pay off:

  Get a new zero per cent card, divide the debt by the number of months the offer lasts and pay it off over that period. Cut up the card on receipt.

- If you have a very big debt to pay off:

  Get a new transfer card offering a low rate for as long as the debt needs to be paid off. Pay it off as a regular amount each month. Cut up the card on receipt.

- If you have poor credit history:

  Do not get a credit card! It probably got you into trouble last time. And the ones you can get will be very expensive.

How not to use your credit card

- Never use it to withdraw cash …

  … unless you are desperate and it really is the only way. And pay it off as soon as you can – it's expensive!

- Never use store cards.

  Cut them up and pay them off.

- Avoid using a credit card abroad. Or get a Nationwide card.

■ Bank loans

> A bank is a place that will lend you money if you can prove that you
> don't need it.   *Bob Hope*

Credit cards are great for short-term debt, balancing income and expenditure
for a few months. But if you want to borrow over a year or more then they
are generally poor value. If you need to borrow £1000 to £15,000 over a
fixed period of one to five years – and that means, of course, you are going
to use the money to buy something that will last that long – then a bank loan
is often the cheapest deal around.

How they work

You borrow between £1000 and £15,000 from the bank. You do not normally have to say what it is for and they never check what you do with it
anyway. You agree to repay it at so much a month for the life of the loan,
normally over one to five years. Your monthly payment has two parts. First,
you have to repay the amount you have borrowed. Secondly, you have to pay
the interest – the amount the bank charges to lend you the money. The bank
will not separate your payment into those two parts. It will just tell you the
monthly repayment. For the best deals you will have to agree to repay it by
direct debit from your current account. That's a good idea anyway, to make
sure you don't miss any payments. But make sure you always have enough
money to meet the payments. Otherwise your bank will bounce the direct
debit and you will be hit by a double whammy of penalties: from the bank
with your current account and from the bank you've borrowed from. And,
yes, they might be the same bank!

Lending money is now big business. And there is fierce competition.
That means that the cheapest loans on the High Street (and internet) are very
cheap indeed. But for some reason, the big banks remain expensive. At one
end of the High Street is Northern Rock, which will lend £5000 over three
years at 5.9 per cent to people with a good credit record. The cost of the
interest is £458. At the other end of the High Street, HSBC will charge you a
whopping £1072 for the same deal, which is an interest rate of 13.9 per cent.
So, when I wrote this in the summer of 2004, you could save more than £600

just by walking from one High Street bank to another. If you worry about understanding interest rates and percentages – don't! All you need remember is to pick the smallest if you're borrowing and the largest if you are saving.

How they trick you

The less you borrow, the higher the interest rate This is true of almost all the banks but, as an example from summer 2004, with Barclays you pay 9.9 per cent if you borrow £5000 but 12.9 per cent if you borrow less. That means that it can end up cheaper to borrow slightly more. For example, if you borrow £4900 over three years, you pay 12.9 per cent and your monthly payments are £163.21. If you borrow £5000, the rate comes down to 9.9 per cent and the monthly repayments are £160.42. So you borrow an extra £100 but pay a couple of pounds a month less and end up paying £100 less in interest over the life of the loan. This trick only works if what you really want to borrow is close to the boundary where the interest rate falls. Don't be fooled into borrowing more than you need because the interest rate is lower.

The shorter the period, the less you pay in interest You cannot normally borrow for less than one year or for more than five or, at the most, seven. Of course, the longer the period, the more interest you end up paying. For example, if you borrow £5000 and pay it back over one year, you'll pay £264 in interest. If you borrow over three years, that rises to £775 in interest. And over five years it costs you £1316 in interest.

You are fined if you pay the loan off early If you lent a friend £20 to the end of the month but she paid you back the next day, you'd probably be pleased. Not the banks. They fine you. It's as if your friend said, 'Oh, Shell, I've got some money off my mum so here's that £20 I owe you,' and you replied, 'Thanks. But as you've paid me back early I'd like another 25p please!' But it seems logical to the banks and other lenders. Normally, if you pay off a loan early you will be charged two months' interest. So if you borrow £5000 over three years at 9.9 per cent and repay it early, you would be charged £43. However, some banks do not make any charge.

Insurance Borrowing is cheap because competition has forced prices down. But the banks are getting more of our money by selling us insurance as well as the loan. This insurance is supposed to protect our payments if we fall sick or lose our jobs and cannot meet the repayments. But it is expensive – more than doubling the cost of borrowing the money – and in many cases it will not pay out anyway. Suppose you borrow £5000 over three years from Egg (which is fairly middling as far as interest rates are concerned). In mid 2004, it was charging £612 in interest to borrow the money. And then charging you £823 to insure your payments.

You can get insurance cheaper than that – Nationwide, for example, charges just £497. But Birmingham Midshires charges a whopping £1371, nearly three times as much. And it does make a difference. Take Egg. It offers a reasonable rate of interest – 7.9 per cent – but if you add on the cost of insurance that shoots up to 18.6 per cent.

The insurance is supposed to meet your payments if you are ill and cannot work or if you are unemployed. Many banks stick in extra life insurance as well, so the debt is paid if you die. But most of these policies don't work for people over pensionable age or who are self-employed. And they also have many restrictions on unemployed people and those who fall sick. Remember, if you are sick, you may well get full or half pay for six months from your employer. Or you may have a partner who can pay. And as for life insurance, most of us have too much of that anyway. But with profit margins estimated at 70 per cent or more, no wonder it's heavily sold.

When you ask a bank for a quote it will *always* include the insurance unless you ask it not to. The bank will seldom tell you the restrictions – unemployed people may only get help for a year, for example. And the cost of the insurance is *excluded* from the APR (annual percentage rate) and the total cost for credit. This is allowed because the insurance is 'optional'. Although research has found that seven out of ten people taking out a loan with one major High Street bank also go for the insurance.

If you are tempted to buy it, find out how much it will pay out and under what circumstances. Consider if those are likely to apply to you and, if they did, whether repaying the loan would be that difficult. If you really do want to be insured, look at the total cost and find the cheapest loans, including insurance. At the moment the cheapest deal for a £5000 loan over three years is £996 for interest and insurance. The dearest on the High Street is £2518, over £1500 more expensive. Now that's money down the drain.

■ Other loans

When you buy anything worth more than about £50 – from a microwave to a new sofa – the shop selling it to you might try to lend you the money to buy it. These deals all work in much the same way as a bank loan but generally are much more expensive. It's usually better to get a bank loan and use the money to buy what you want. Shops will also try to make more money out of you by selling you insurance.

Some loans you take out in shops and garages are what's called hire purchase (HP). This is an old-fashioned sort of credit. Although HP agreements still have to tell you the total charge for credit and the APR, unlike with conventional credit agreements, you don't actually own the item until you make the final payment. If you have paid less than one-third of the price of the item, the lender can repossess it without going to court (though not in Scotland).

If you are offered credit in a shop or garage, look carefully at the deal. You will sometimes be offered zero per cent credit, but that may hide the fact that the price quoted is higher than it should be. The most important thing is the APR. If that is more than about 10 per cent, then the deal is too dear and you should think of another way of paying for the item.

■ Overdrafts

I must become a borrower of the night, for a dark hour or twain

Banquo in Macbeth III 1 26

Next to your credit card, an overdraft is probably the simplest way to get into expensive debt. Like credit cards, overdrafts can be useful. The flexibility to spend a bit more than you earn, or at least spend it a short time before you are paid, is useful. And tempting. The trouble is that once you have used it, the temptation is to see the overdraft as your money, and to see the cost of it on your bank statement each month as just one of life's little overheads.

The banks don't help. They offer a small 'comfort zone' overdraft that can range from £100 to as much as £1000, which is automatic and sometimes even interest-free. But these generous offers can make an overdraft seem 'normal'. Which it shouldn't be. Because once you go over these limits, the charges can be very high.

There are two sorts of overdraft. One sort is bad. The other is evil. The bad sort is the overdraft you agree with your bank. Nowadays you may well be offered an overdraft facility when you open the account. In other words, the bank will let you go overdrawn by a certain amount without penalties. But even these penalty-free overdrafts can put you through the wringer. Take the Co-operative Bank. I was shocked when I researched their fees in 2004 to find that it charges three times for an agreed overdraft.

> **Charge 1** First it charges you £15 to arrange an overdraft at all. You say, 'Can I have a £1000 overdraft facility please?' The bank says yes and whips £15 off the money in your current account.
>
> **Charge 2** It then charges you a fee of £8 each month you use the overdraft. In other words, you get paid on the 28th, but a day earlier, on 27th, you go overdrawn by a few pounds and you get charged £8.
>
> **Charge 3** Finally, it charges you 19.56 per cent interest on the money you owe – the highest rate of interest on an authorized overdraft on the High Street.

For example, suppose you arrange a £500 overdraft and you use it on average for ten days a month and average £250 overdrawn. At the end of a year you will have paid £126 in charges. That's equivalent to an APR of around 348 per cent each month. For an agreed overdraft!

Thankfully, not all banks are this bad. Only a handful charge for agreeing the overdraft (although those that do can charge up to £25). And another handful charge a monthly usage fee of up to £9.50 a month. All the rest just charge interest. And that ranges from the horrific 19.56 per cent to a reasonable 6.75 per cent (Nationwide). The overdraft pattern described in the previous paragraph would cost you £5.42 in interest over a year with Nationwide, though this is a saving of at least £120 compared to its more expensive rival.

Although Nationwide has the lowest overdraft rate as I write this, it's not quite the cheapest option. Even cheaper is cahoot, which allows you to go up to £250 overdrawn without charging a penny in interest. Depending on how you use the account, the same £500 facility would probably cost you just £2.25 during the course of the year.

So, if you go overdrawn regularly, switching to a bank that has cheaper overdrafts will save you a lot. If your bank charges you to agree an overdraft or a monthly fee for using it, switch banks.

If you think these overdrafts are bad, and on the whole they are, then prepare to be afraid, very afraid. They have got nothing on the 'evil' overdrafts. Or perhaps this is unfair. Perhaps it is customers who are wicked if they take money out of their account that's not there and without permission. As I said earlier, this could be called theft. In France it is, and you face a loss of facilities at all French banks! Here, they just charge you loads of money. So if you are going to go overdrawn you should warn the bank and agree to borrow the money first. After all, if you needed a loan from your best friend you would ask first rather than just raiding her purse, wouldn't you? If you do not ask your bank before going overdrawn, it will punish you severely. Not only is the rate of interest sky-high, you are also charged hefty penalties every time you breathe. Here are some of their tactics.

Letter They write to you and charge you up to £13 a time. So if they wrote each month for a year, it could cost you up to £156.

Daily fee Up to £20 a day. Lloyds TSB charges this but caps it at £80 a month, so maximum of £960 a year.

Monthly fee Usually, but not always, an alternative to the daily fee – up to £28 a month or £336 a year.

Transaction fee Each time you go more overdrawn, they charge you up to £25. Over a year that could be anything, but if it were to happen twice a month for a year, that would be £600.

Interest rate Up to 33.8 per cent. So for an overdraft of £500 over a year, you pay £169.

So if you went up to £500 overdrawn, without permission, each month for a year you could end up paying £1000 in charges to borrow £500.

To take the example of the Co-operative Bank – which may not be the most expensive for unauthorized overdrafts – if you go up to £500 overdrawn each month without permission, and only write one cheque a month that makes you overdrawn, you would end up paying more than £500 a year in charges and the APR would work out at around 321 per cent.

So while there are good deals around – Nationwide or cahoot for authorized overdrafts and Barclays for unauthorized ones – there are also some banks for which the word 'usury' could have been invented. In fact, it probably was. (Usury, noun, the practice of lending money at an exorbitant, excessive or illegal rate, although, of course, there is no rate of interest that is actually illegal in the UK.) Avoid them.

And if you cannot avoid going overdrawn, do it very carefully. And tear up a £10 note from time to time just to remind yourself what you are doing with your money.

■ The credit crunch

Credit is at the heart of the UK economy. It keeps the banks in business, it keeps the shop tills ringing, and it means we can all have what we want when we want it. All thanks to instant credit. Decisions whether or not to lend us money are made in seconds. How?

Every one of us has a credit record stored on computer at three companies called credit reference agencies. They all do much the same job and most retailers and banks subscribe to their services. They keep information on us from us three sources:

- Public information, which includes the list of names and addresses of adults who are entitled to vote, and court records of cases involving debt and bankruptcy.
- Information from credit companies, including details of any credit cards you have, loans, mobile and fixed phones and some gas, electricity and water companies where you pay monthly.
- Details of any other people or addresses you have a financial connection with.

They use the details of who is entitled to vote because it's the most complete list of names and addresses in the UK. The electoral roll, as it's known, is kept by your local council. It's fully revised once a year and updated monthly. The data is used to confirm that you live where you say you do. When you fill in the annual form for the electoral roll there is a box to tick that prevents the information you have given being used for commercial purposes. Around one in five people do tick that box. But it does not stop the information being passed on to the credit reference agencies. They are given it whether you tick or not. So if the voting list doesn't show you at the address where you live, you may have problems getting credit.

The court system provides information about all cases involving debt or bankruptcy. So anyone who is taken to court over a debt and fails to pay it off before a judgement is given against them will be recorded. These records are kept for six years. Similarly, if you go personally bankrupt then your name will stay on the credit database for six years. That applies even though you can get 'discharged' from bankruptcy after 12 months.

All the companies that subscribe to the database also provide it with information. So your record will show your credit cards, loan agreements, and even bills like phone and utility ones if you pay monthly. Technically this is a 'credit' agreement because you are billed and then pay later. The information will show how much you owe and there will be a code showing how up-to-date your payments are.

The information about other addresses or other people you are linked to is one of the most controversial parts of the database. In the past people with the same surnames and addresses have been 'linked' and financial data on all of them stored together. That changed in 2004 and now your record should only show people or addresses you have a direct financial link with, such as a joint loan or mortgage.

The credit reference agencies which store this data take no responsibility for its accuracy. Technically, the data belongs to the companies that provide it. And only they can correct it. So if you think the information about you is wrong you can tell the credit reference agency, but to get it corrected you will have to go back to the company that provided it. Only if it agrees to the change will it be corrected on your credit file. You can, however, put a 'notice of correction' – up to 200 words correcting or explaining details – on your credit file. For more on credit reference agencies, see Follow-up, page 204.

If the words 'data protection' and 'personal privacy' are coming to mind, you may wonder how these agencies are allowed to store all this information on you. The answer is simple. You gave them permission! Every time you take out a credit card or a loan or arrange to pay for your phone or gas bill every month, you will sign a form and somewhere in the small print will be your permission for them to share the information about your account in this way. You don't have to give permission. But if you refuse, you won't get the credit.

The information on your credit file is used every time you apply for credit. Each bank or lender has its own way of using it to give you what is called a credit score. So there is no single 'credit score' which is 'yours' and which every lender will use. The credit reference agencies do not process the information or score you. They just keep the data. And refuse to take the blame for things going wrong.

However, in response to public demand – and seeing a way to make money – the major credit reference agencies will tell you what they think your credit score is likely to be. This service is not cheap and, at the moment, is of limited use. There is nothing to show how you can improve your credit score. And even the agencies admit these scores will not tell you whether or not you will or will not get credit from a particular lender. Each lender calculates its own credit score, and you can even get a different score for different products. This process happens in seconds – you can take out a store card, arrange hire purchase or make a credit deal in a shop without waiting. Or not. Because it is just as quick, and just as definite, to be refused credit on the spot as it is to be given it. If you are refused, then waving your credit score at them is not likely to get them to change their minds. You can ask them why they refused you but the answer is unlikely to be helpful.

How people are 'scored' is a process surrounded in secrecy. But we do know that companies also use the information on your application form for credit, and any other information they may hold about you – if you are an existing or previous customer, for example.

The best thing to do is to get a copy of your credit file from the credit reference agencies and work it out yourself. They are obliged to supply you with a copy for £2 – though they all will offer you more services and try to charge you extra for them. Things that may count against you, and where the information comes from, include:

- You have been bankrupt or had a court judgement for debt (public records).
- You rent rather than own your home (application form).
- You have come to agreements in the past to write off debt or pay it off under special arrangements (credit reference agency).
- You have moved a lot (application form and public records).
- You often pay your loan or credit card bills late (credit reference agency).
- You have no credit deals so they cannot judge what you are like (credit reference agency).
- You have put a notice of correction on the form (credit reference agency). This notice has to be read and considered, and that cannot be done by a computer. So it will stop any application for instant credit. But it may mean that you finally do get the credit you want if you apply, for example, by post or online.
- You have a mobile phone but not a fixed-line one (application form).
- The bank thinks you will pay things off perfectly on time and so it will earn very little money from you (credit reference agency; bank's own records).

Not every one of these reasons will be used by every lender every time. And none of them will be an absolute bar to credit. Even discharged bankrupts can get loans from some companies, though they pay a heavy price in high interest rates. It also means there is no 'credit blacklist' that stops you getting credit from everyone under all circumstances. But if you have a bad score, you have a bad score, and that will make getting credit at a fair price more difficult. And it will rather limit you if you want to be a rate tart, and get lots of credit cards and do clever things with them.

You will see adverts by companies that offer to 'repair' your credit record if you pay them a fee. They cannot do it and should be avoided. If there are mistakes on your record or the information on it is old and should have run out, then you can get the record changed for nothing. If the record is accurate, then it is not possible to change it.

Risk-based pricing

Banks have recently started using credit scores in a different way. Instead of just saying yes or no to credit, they will charge people with bad scores more. Barclaycard, for example, charges customers between 11.9 per cent and 24.9 per cent on any outstanding debt. The customers who are the biggest 'risk' are charged the highest rates. This may include people who just have no credit record at all. So it's a sort of 'starter' rate. All those with a poor credit score for whatever reason will pay more.

That need not be a bad thing. If you have a poor credit score, then getting any card may be better than getting no card at all. And once you have proved you are a good risk, the rate you pay may be cut, especially if you ask. But it does mean that you have to be careful of adverts that seem to offer very low rates 'from' a certain amount. With a poor credit record you may end up paying twice as much as the advertised rate.

■ Student debt

If you are under about 30 and went to university you probably have student debt. It does seem a strange way to organize the world – giving half the population debts of more than £12,000 when they start out in life. But although that is a lot of money, student debt is quite good debt. The interest rate is fixed at the rate of inflation in the March before the start of the academic year in September. So in the 2004 new academic year it was 2.6 per cent.

Unless you have no other debt, it is probably as well to allow the student loan to be paid off in its own time. There is no point in struggling to pay off a debt at 2.6 per cent and then finding you have to borrow at three or even ten times that rate or more when you need money in the future. People who start university in September 2006 or later will have any outstanding debt written off after 25 years. Most people pay off their student loan out of their pay automatically once their salary is above a certain amount.

In itself, having a student loan should not affect your ability to borrow money. But it will affect the income you have available to repay a loan, and could affect the amount you can borrow, including the amount you can borrow on a mortgage. Especially one worked out on your ability to pay rather than just a multiple of your income.

■ Home-secured loans

If you are a home owner and you have a poor credit record or want to borrow a lot of money over more than five years, you may be tempted to take out a loan from a debt consolidation company that is 'secured' on your home. It might be the only loan that is available and it will certainly seem cheaper than some of the alternatives. But be very careful. If a loan is secured on your home it means that if you miss payments the lender can take your home, throw you out and sell it at auction to recover the money you owe. So it is not a step to be taken lightly. It is this security for the lender that makes these loans cheaper. If you do not pay back a personal loan or a credit card debt, the bank has to go to court to recover the money owed. This is time-consuming and expensive, and ultimately the bank may not recover the money. With a secured loan, your home is worth much more than the loan and the company is taking little risk. Of course, there will be legal processes to go through – all of which you will end up paying for – but ultimately the company knows it can get its money back.

▌ THE GOLDEN RULE OF LOANS

■ Borrowing to pay off a loan is not paying off a loan

Sometimes these loans are marketed cleverly. 'Clear your debts and cut your monthly payments in half!'

So how can they pay off all your debts *and* cut your payments in half? In two ways. First, they secure the debt on your home. (There's less risk, so interest rates are lower.) Second, they lend you the money over a longer period. Some of them offer to lend you money over what they call '300 months'.

That's 25 years. So if your credit cards and other loans were for things like holidays, clothes, household things, maybe even the odd grocery bill on your unpaid credit card, you will be paying those back over 25 years! Not a good idea. Although your monthly payments will be lower, the amount you pay for interest over those years will be much higher. For example, if you borrow £20,000 at 8.4 per cent over 120 months (aka 10 years) you will end up paying more than £9000 in interest. And if you miss payments the loan company can ultimately repossess your home. Neither is very attractive when put like that, is it?

So avoid debt consolidation companies. They make the Black Death look like a friend of humankind.

■ Debt problems and help

Debt problems start slowly. You spend a bit more than you earn. The credit card debt builds up. Maybe you take out a bank loan to pay it off. But you start using the card again. And the debt grows. You might not even know exactly how much it is. But what with paying off your loans and your household bills, there's not much left at the end of the month, so you start using your credit card earlier in the month. At this stage you dread coming home each night to face the bills. And a lot of us, when faced with this situation, have one reaction. We don't open them. I would say we bury our heads in the sand, except that ostriches would sue. Because they don't do that. Ever.

It is the worst thing to do.

Imagine you lend a friend at work £20. She promises to pay you back at the end of the week when she is paid. Friday comes and she says nothing to you, seems to avoid you. You spend the weekend worrying. On Monday it's the same. Instead of emailing you about her weekend and maybe calling, she is silent. When you do see her in the corridor, she pretends not to see you and walks the other way. Now you are really worried. And you start to talk to some of your other friends, telling them that she owes you £20 and has not paid you back. What's wrong with her? No one knows. The truth is, poor Jane has had a difficult time. She did get paid, but the night before that her dog had been hit by a car and she had to pay the vet on the spot and she has, literally, no money left to pay you. How much better if she had told you that right away. You would have been sympathetic. But because she hid and went silent, you got suspicious. I won't say banks are human. But they do behave like us sometimes. Hiding and going silent is not the way to deal with people – or banks – you owe money to. Time for a Golden Rule.

THE GOLDEN RULE OF DEBT

■ Never ignore your debts

If you do, they will not go away. They will only get worse. If you cannot meet your bills, then tell the people you owe money to. They may not seem sympathetic. In fact, they might seem horrid. But it's still much better to tell them. The Golden Rule with debt is never ignore it. Creditors would rather hear bad news from you than nothing at all.

But before telling them, be honest with yourself. If you are that worried, you probably don't know the extent of what you owe. And if you cannot be honest with yourself, how can you be honest with other people?

So sort out all the bits of paper that show what you owe. If you have thrown some away – perhaps even unopened – then sort out what you have left and estimate the missing ones. You can always get copies, especially if you do your banking on the internet. Collect them all, sort them into date order, add up what you owe – and what you should pay back each month. Swallow. Breathe hard. Read on.

Some debts are more important than others. Some just *have* to be paid. If you are a home owner, your mortgage is the first priority, along with any other debts you have secured on your home. Failing to pay either of these can mean your home may be repossessed. If you are not a home owner, then your rent is top priority. After that comes council tax – you can be jailed if you don't pay it. And the same is true of any fines you owe to a court.

Next come your electricity and gas bills. If you do not pay these, you may end up being disconnected. At best you will be moved to a more expensive tariff where you have to charge up an electronic key with cash when your power runs out.

If you are being threatened with court action over your debts, then those debts should also be given priority, partly because you will avoid court costs, which can be high, and partly because if you get a judgement against you it will make getting credit much more difficult in the future.

Then look at all your other debts – credit cards, store cards, bank loans, hire purchase agreements, credit agreements with shops, phone bills, cable or satellite TV bills and so on. Write down the debts that have the highest rates of interest – if you don't know which they are, then that's part of what has gone wrong. It should be on a piece of paper somewhere. If you have thrown it away, call the company and ask.

So much for your debts. Now look at your income. Write down what you have coming in each month.

Then take off things you have to pay out each month – mortgage or rent, electricity, gas, fares to work – and allow something for food and for one telephone. These are the amounts you have to pay each month, not the debt you may have built up.

What's left is the amount you can afford to start paying off your debts. Deal with them in the priority list you drew up above – first, things that let you stay in your home, then the ones where jail or court action is threatened, then the debts with the highest interest rates.

All this may sound very depressing. But, in fact, it can give you a great sense of relief. You will have taken the first step in dealing with something that has caused you sleepless nights and a sick feeling in your stomach. And once you write everything down and add it all up, the problem may not be as bad as you fear.

Of course, if the problem is too big, then you will have to get help. There are organizations that will offer free sympathetic advice, will not criticize you or judge you and will offer practical help to deal with your creditors. All at no cost to you. They will negotiate with your creditors and get debts frozen so that no more interest is added on, get payments deferred, arrange small payments to start clearing the loans, and even, in some cases, get debts written off. The three free national organizations you should consider are: the Consumer Credit Counselling Service, the National Debtline and your local Citizen's Advice Bureau (see Follow-up, page 205).

There are other companies around that will offer similar help, but they will charge you a fee. If you already owe too much money, the last thing you need to do is spend money on help to get rid of the debt. So avoid them.

Bankruptcy

Of all the ways out of debt, bankruptcy is the nuclear option. A weapon to keep in reserve but not to use except in the most dire circumstances. OK, it's not as horrific as nuclear war. Maybe it's a bit more like war itself – something you might threaten to do and in rare cases might actually do. But not lightly. Because there will be casualties, including you.

If you go bankrupt your debts are written off. That's the good news. But you will have to sell a lot of your possessions to pay what you can off your debts, including any share you may have in the home you live in. For up to three years, some of what you earn will also have to be passed on to help pay off the creditors. (Your pension will normally be safe, as will the basic things you need for your life.) You will also find it very hard to get credit for the next six years, and will not be able to have a normal bank account for at least a year. It will be harder, or at least more expensive, to get gas or electricity supplies and telephone services, and you will have to give up all your credit cards.

After a year you will be what is called 'discharged' from bankruptcy. But that is not the end of the matter. Your credit record will contain the details of your bankruptcy for six years and some of your income may still be taken towards your debts for another two years. Of course, all this might be better than feeling sick all the time and facing the bleak prospect of owing tens of thousands of pounds for ever. So it is worth considering. But not doing lightly.

Paying off debt

Well, that was all a bit scary wasn't it? Maybe things aren't that bad. In which case, you can try a do-it-yourself way of reducing your debt. It's quite simple – though, of course, not necessarily easy – and it uses the power of arithmetic.

I know you always hated them, but percentages are easy. Think of them as pence in the pound. If you have one pound, then 4 per cent of it is 4p. 62 per cent of it is 62p. So if someone is charging you 16 per cent on your loan, for every pound you have borrowed you pay 16 pence a year to them. Multiply all those by 1000. You borrow £1000, the charge is 16 per cent so you pay £160 a year in interest.

Suppose you have debts on three credit cards. Awful Bank charges you 16.9 per cent. Better Inc. charges 11.9 per cent. Cheapasitgets charges 5.9 per cent. I'll call them A, B and C. You owe **A** £1000, **B** £4325 and C £1200.

You are only paying the minimum. One asks for 2 per cent, the others 3 per cent. So you are paying them back like this.

MINIMUM PAYMENTS

Card	Minimum payment	You pay	Time to pay off	Interest paid
Awfulbank (£1000)	2%	£20		
Better inc. (£4325)	3%	£131		
Cheapasitgets (£1200)	3%	£36		

How long do you think it will take you to pay off these debts if you stop using the card and carry on making the minimum payments? And how much interest would you pay over that time? Go on, write them in the table above. And then I want to do what in film or TV they call a 'reveal'. Essentially what it means for you is turning the page. OK, drum roll and REVEAL …

MINIMUM PAYMENTS AND TIME TO PAY OFF

Card	Minimum payment	You pay	Time to pay off	Interest paid
Awfulbank (£1000)	2%	£20	23 years	£1545
Better inc. (£4325)	3%	£131	16 years 3 months	£1911
Cheapasitgets (£1200)	3%	£36	9 years 6 months	£217

Did you get anywhere *near* the right answer? Isn't it frightening? Yes. Can it be avoided? Yes. Here's how.

At the moment you owe Awful Bank £1000 and its minimum payment is 2 per cent so it charges you £20. (Actually, the arithmetic is a bit more complicated than this but let's ignore that.) But next month you will owe it a little bit less, so it will charge you 2 per cent of that, which might be £19.83 and so on. Eventually, you will owe it around £250 and the minimum payment will be £5 and it sticks there until it is paid off. Otherwise your debt would go on almost for ever. The high interest rate and the low minimum means this is a debt that sticks around.

But here's a simple trick. Change your standing order so that instead of paying the minimum, you take the £20 you are paying this month and double it. Then pay that amount every month. Come on, it's only another £20. You can afford it. Then your debt will disappear in 2 years 7 months, and you will only pay £225 in interest. With the other two, convert them to a fixed amount too. But this time fix them at the current minimum payment. So you pay £131 a month to Better Inc and £36 to Cheapasitgets. If you left it at that you would pay off Better inc after 3 years 4 months and Cheapetc in a couple of months less. So in three years you could be free of debt. Even better, when the Awfulbank payments stop, move that £40 to the next dearest, Better Inc., and add that on so you pay £171 a month and that will get you out of debt in just three years.

Now three years may sound a long time. But what a goal! Debt-free! If you don't do this, you could be in debt for the rest of your life. But if you do, you could be debt-free for ever. Money magic!

GOLDEN RULE OF CLEARING DEBT

■ Forget minimum payments; pay a fixed amount each month until it's gone

■ Buying a home

If there's one area where money magic produces rapid results, it is our mortgage. If you don't have one (chance would be a fine thing, I can hear many younger readers, whose pay is a small fraction of the cheapest home on the market where they live, snorting), read on anyway. Not least because the general principles will apply when you do feel you can take on a mortgage, and also because you might even discover that you are in a better position than you thought.

■ Changing mortgage

Changing your mortgage can save you thousands of pounds over the next few years. Not many financial changes match it in the quantity or speed of the results. Most of us stick with the same mortgage we have had since we bought our home. But that can be a very expensive mistake. Millions of home owners are wasting a thousand pounds a year or more by doing nothing.

Even though interest rates are rising, mortgages are still fabulous value. In continental Europe where the official rate of interest is much lower – less than half what it is in the UK – the cost of borrowing to buy a home is no cheaper, and can be more expensive. It comes back to competition. And the fact that we love a bargain. The banks are desperate to get our business, and to get it they are making us offers we should not refuse. The result is a fantastic but completely baffling choice. But don't let that put you off. Just look at the figures. If you have a £100,000 loan and you're paying the standard sort of interest rate – say 6.25 per cent – then there are risk-free deals around that will save you £188 a month. And if your mortgage is twice as big, the savings are doubled.

Here is how it works. That rate of 6.25 per cent interest is fairly typical for what the lenders call the 'standard variable rate', or SVR. A better term would be 'bog standard deal'. So if you borrow £100,000 and are on the bog standard deal, you will pay £6250 a year – £520 a month – in interest alone. And if it's a repayment mortgage your payments will be higher than that – around £660 a month. Suppose you can cut the interest to 3.99 per cent. You would save £2260 a year or £188 a month on an interest-free mortgage, or £132 a month on a repayment mortgage. Think what you could do with that! And it's not a dream. It can be done.

If you are on the bog standard mortgage deal, you are probably wasting at least £1000 a year.

These good mortgage deals only last for a limited time. The 3.99 per cent, for example, only lasts for two years. After that your mortgage rate will go back to 6.25 per cent. So two years from now you will have to pay more – or find the current deal of the day then and switch again. It's a mad way to run things, but that's how it is. Only the foolish, the lazy, the ignorant – and those with a bad credit record – pay the full amount for a mortgage. And the rate tarts prosper.

Over the two-year life of the deal you will have saved more than £4500. If you use that to pay some of what you owe on your mortgage, then you will reap the benefits of that for the rest of your life. This saving applies to people with an interest-only mortgage – the sort you have with an endowment or savings plan to pay off the capital at the end of the mortgage. But even if you have a repayment mortgage – where your monthly payments go towards paying off some of the capital as well as the interest – the savings are nearly as big: around £132 a month, or £3174 over two years.

The snag is that you are locked into the deal for two years, and you can't change if a better deal comes along. Or if you do, the lender will fine you, possibly by taking back all the savings you have made. But once the two years are up, and the monthly savings stop, then you are free to look around.

Sorry, but we are now going to have to use a bit of jargon. The deal just described is called a 'discounted variable rate'. What does that mean? 'Rate' is easy: it's the percentage you are charged (3.99 per cent). 'Variable' means it varies. As the Bank of England puts interest rates up and down, yours will go up and down too. And 'discounted' is the bit you save. This one cuts 2.26 per cent off the bog standard deal. Hence discounted, variable rate. And it does that for two years.

It's a fix!

There are other deals. One of the most popular is the fixed-rate mortgage. Again, that means what it says – the rate is fixed for a set period. Two and five years are the most common periods, but you can fix it for up to 25 years if you want.

Fixed-rate mortgages suit people who want to know what their monthly repayments will be. Perhaps you're fed up with the Bank of England changing the rate of interest every few months and your mortgage repayments going up and down. Or maybe you mortgaged yourself to the hilt to buy that dream home and you just have to know that your repayments won't shoot up if interest rates rise again. Either way a fixed rate may suit you because it guarantees the rate of interest will not change over the fixed period.

Fixed rates are a gamble. If interest rates carry on rising, you're in the money. But if they fall you can find yourself paying more than the going rate. And almost all fixed-rate deals impose a big penalty on customers who try to get out before the end of the fixed-rate period. Some will charge a penalty even after that, locking you in for years on what might be a high interest rate. These should be avoided. But if you can find a fixed rate around 1 per cent less than the standard mortgage rate, with no penalties if you leave the deal once the fixed rate period is over, then that could be the one to go for.

For example, there is a mortgage around at the moment offering 5.39 per cent for five years. If you are on the bog standard deal that will save you £860 a year, around £71 a month. Enough for a holiday for two once a year!

If rates stay the same you will save that for 60 months – a total of £4300. At the moment rates are expected to rise (though by the time you read this, things being what they are, that may have changed). If they do, you will save even more. If they fall, you will end up with a mortgage that seems expensive. But the most important thing is that you know you can afford your mortgage payments for at least the next five years.

If, like me, you're not a gambler, then consider the fixed rate's close relative, the 'cap'. With these one-way bets the rate of interest can go down any amount; but the lender guarantees it will never go up beyond a certain level – the cap. Generally you are unlikely to do as well with a cap as on a fixed rate. But it does protect you if rates shoot up.

You have to weigh up the choice yourself. Do you want a slightly bigger discount but run the risk of a big penalty if you suddenly want to pay off the mortgage or move it somewhere else? Myself I prefer flexibility. Who knows what the world – or your life – will be like in the spring of 2007? Or 2012?

Tracking device

One alternative to a discounted rate is a tracker mortgage. This type of mortgage is guaranteed to be a fixed percentage above the base rate set by the Bank of England. So you know that as the base rate changes, so will your mortgage – but not by any more than the change in the base rate.

In the past some lenders took advantage of rising base rates by putting up mortgage rates by even more than the rise the bank announced. But nowadays it is very unlikely that a lender will rack up the rate by more than the Bank of England change – though some do cut them by less when rates go down. Trackers are probably better in an environment where rates are falling.

The cost of changing

Two things put people off changing their mortgage. One is not knowing how to do it (which is why most borrowers now go to a mortgage broker for help). And the other is the cost. And it's true that changing does mean spending some cash up front.

There are four charges you might face.

Valuation Your new lender will want to make sure your home is worth more than the new mortgage.

Solicitor You will need one to arrange the legal stuff.

Arrangement Some lenders charge a fee for arranging the loan – a real cheek. It's as if Dixons were to sell you a television and then add on a fee for selling it you!

Adviser If you use a mortgage adviser they will normally make a charge for the advice and sorting out the deal.

Reckon on up to £300 for each of the first three of these costs. And the arrangement fee is creeping up. Some lenders can charge £500 for that. The mortgage adviser may be more – up to 1 per cent of the loan. So your first year's savings could be swallowed up at once. But you can get all these things free if you look around.

Lenders will sometimes pay for the valuation or the legal fees. Some lenders – the good guys – do not charge an arrangement fee. And some brokers even work for nothing. Well, not quite. They all get paid by the lender for putting the new business their way. But most also charge you, which, again, is a bit of a cheek. But do remember that good advice you pay for is much better than bad advice you get free. And one thing is certain. The most expensive thing to do with your mortgage is almost certainly to do nothing.

Flexible lends

Variable, tracker, fixed – or capped – is not the only choice you can make. Most mortgages nowadays are 'flexible'. That means you can pay extra amounts off the debt if you can afford it, and borrow it back later if you need it. Or you can miss a payment if things get really tough (though please, please only do that as a last resort!). You may be surprised this is all such a big deal. But in the past, you had to pay a certain amount each month and if you paid less or more then you could be fined. And when you did pay more, the extra was not used to reduce your debt – and the interest due – for up to a year.

So check two things – is the interest calculated every day, or at least once a month rather than once a year? Avoid once a year like the plague. Second, can you overpay when you want to and get it back if you need it?

Third, can you miss a payment from time to time without a penalty? But, of course, when you do miss a payment your debt and the interest charged on it will be that much more.

Offset mortgages

The ultimate in flexibility are what are called current account mortgages or offset mortgages. To understand this impenetrable bit of jargon, let's take a step back.

You have a current account. Your pay goes in each month and you slowly use it – or more – over the next 30 days. You also have a small amount of savings, plus, say, a credit card or a bank loan. And you have a mortgage. The money in your current account might earn as little as 0.1 per cent or as much as 4 per cent, depending where it is (see Bank charges, page 46). If you go overdrawn, you are charged. Your savings account might earn 3 to 5 per cent. Your credit card is charging you 14.9 per cent on what you owe. Your bank loan is 9.9 per cent and your overdraft for the days you have one is 14.9 per cent. Your mortgage is 6.25 per cent. It's all a bit mad. You are in credit on one account earning almost nothing, but in debit on others paying a variety of rates of interest.

A current account mortgage tidies all this up. Here's how it works. You put all your finances with one bank. So your mortgage, credit card, loan and current account are all with the same bank. Each day the bank adds up all the money you have in your current and savings account, and takes off all your debts, including your loan, your credit card debt and your mortgage. The difference is what you owe. And they charge you one low mortgage rate on it. So, as your pay goes in each month, your debts and the interest you pay is reduced. Over the month, your debt grows and the interest is slightly more.

This system has two big advantages. First, you are paying less on your debt. It's effectively all treated like a mortgage – but don't worry, apart from your home loan, it is not 'secured' on your home. Second, every penny you have in your current and savings account is reducing your debt – in effect, earning interest at the rate of your mortgage. But these arrangements do not suit everybody. And should be kept under review to make sure they continue to save you money.

Answer to the question on page 110: There are, in fact, three cheaper forms of debt than a mortgage. So, well done if you got two of them. They are (a) an interest-free credit card, (b) a low-interest balance transfer credit card and (c) a student loan.

Prediction is very difficult, especially if it is about the future.

Nils Bohr

Chapter 7
Saving for the future

❏ Saving and investing

❏ Different plans for different stages

❏ How does money grow, and why?

❏ Risk

❏ Protecting your money

❏ Getting good financial advice

What is the difference between saving and investing? Ask most financial advisers that and they won't have clue. Ask Her Majesty's Treasury and it will confuse you by calling an investment a 'savings account'. Ask National Savings & Investments – which should surely know as it has both words in its name – and you will end up more confused than ever. But there is one very simple difference between saving and investing. If you save, then your money remains yours. If you invest, then your money belongs to someone else.

It's that simple. And that important. Put this on a Post-It note before you go looking to put your money somewhere.

IF YOU SAVE, YOUR MONEY REMAINS YOURS.
IF YOU INVEST, YOUR MONEY BELONGS TO SOMEONE ELSE.

Suppose you have £500 to spare. You go to the bank and put it into a savings account. The £500 remains yours. You have lent it to the bank. A year later, you need the money back. You go along to the bank and take it out and, hey, the bank has added £20. It takes off £4 tax, which leaves you with a profit of £16. And you have done no work! Money magic!

Alternatively, you go to Mr Oldenshaw's antique shop. You see a really nice antique chair for £550. You bargain with Mr Oldenshaw and hand over £500 in 50 crisp tenners. He gives you the chair. You take it home and sit on it. A year later, you need the money back. You cannot take the chair to the bank and cash it in. You have to sell it. But Mr Oldenshaw, who really loved that chair and told you how rare a chair of that age was, especially in that condition, now says the market for old chairs has dried up recently and the most he can give you is £300. And that is cutting his own throat. Loss: £200.

There, in a nutshell, is the difference between saving and investing. Many people think that because many things called investments involve money, rather than furniture, the money they use to buy them is still some-how 'theirs'. It isn't. Just like when you buy a chair. The money is someone else's. The investment is yours. And whether you get your money back depends on the seller's honesty when they sell you the investment. And whether someone will want to buy it for the right price when you want to sell it.

Another difference is risk. This little word simply means that there can be a happy ending or a sad ending. And often the difference between them is out of your hands.

We've seen the sad ending with the chair. But there is a happy alternative. You take it to Chairstyle, a specialist dealer. Miss Carver takes one look at it and her eyes light up. She has just the customer, someone who needs your chair to make a nice mixed set of six. After some bargaining you settle on £600. She writes you a cheque and it doesn't bounce. Profit: £100.

So risk goes both ways. Put it in the bank and there is no risk – you know you will make a small amount of money. Buy a chair and there's a chance you will make a lot more money than you would in the bank. But there's also the chance you will *lose* money. That is what risk means. You gamble the chance of making more money against the chance of losing some of the money you invested.

Or even all of it. Here's a third scenario. You take the chair to Hammer & Co., an auction house in the nearest big town. Its English furniture specialist, Mr I. Eagle, looks at it and purses his lips. One front leg has been replaced with a modern reproduction. Good but not original. And he thinks the splats in the back are from another chair of a different date, not fakes but what they call a 'marriage'. Two bits of furniture masquerading as one (though why that's like a marriage I don't know!). Oh, and yes, there is a bit of woodworm in the original front leg and it is a bit wobbly. (You knew that. You thought it was because it was old.) He smiles. He could put it in the sale. But he would not anticipate getting more than £25 for it. And really, if you like it, his advice would be to take it home and sit on it. Carefully. Loss: the lot. All £500.

With any definition there are borderline cases. And people will invent them to confuse you. But if you stick to your guns, you can rely on the definition on the Post-It. It will help you through this chapter, this book and your life.

▓ What are you saving for?

Save for the time, not the purpose. It doesn't matter what you are saving for. What matters is: when will you need it? Whether you are buying a coat, a car, a holiday, a house or a pension is irrelevant. But *when* you will need the money is crucial to deciding how you will save for it. Because *when* you need the money affects *where* you should put it.

I divide 'when' into four categories. There are no official categories and mine tend to be a bit different from the ones the financial services industry uses. That's because the products they want you to buy are the ones that pay the best commission. And those are the ones that are riskier and tend to be sold for longer-term investments. My four categories, then, are as follows.

Immediate

In other words, less than one year. Examples: Christmas, holiday, new coat, birthday party, piece of furniture, computer, general reserve money.

For something you need in less than one year there is only one choice: a good instant-access cash savings account, preferably one where you do not pay tax on the interest earned. These are called cash ISAs and there is more about them in Tax-free savings on page 153. If you have already used up your ISA allowance – you have put the full £3000 into one this tax year – then pick the best instant-access account you can find (see Other Savings, page 156).

Work out what you want to buy. Say a holiday. It's September. You're just back from abroad but already thinking about next year's break. The holiday will cost £600. So you have to save up £50 a month from September to July, then with another £50 in August you'll have £600. What's more, the holidays that cost £700 or £800 to book ahead in January will then be available at a lower cost when you walk in waving your debit card. Now you may say, 'I can't afford £50 a month!' Then I reply, 'Well, you cannot afford this holiday.' It has to be paid for. If it's your only holiday of the year then the most you can pay it back over is 12 months (see Golden Rule of Borrowing, page 110).

Here is the alternative. Suppose you pay for it next August with a credit card. And you are really disciplined and pay it back over 12 months. That will cost you £54.61 a month to clear it over a year. That's £600 for your holiday and £55 in interest. If you save up for it, you will have to save £49 a month and that, with the £12 interest you will earn, makes £600. So you are £67 better off. Can't be bothered? OK. Go to the nearest cash machine, draw out £60, rummage in your pocket or purse for a fiver and two pound coins, and throw them away. Or better still, post them to me, care of the publishers. That's what it's like. Throwing away money.

If you cannot open an ISA – perhaps you have one already – then you can earn a bit more interest in an account where you commit yourself to saving a regular amount each month. But you must be convinced that, come what may, you will be able to save that guaranteed amount. If you're not sure, then pick the highest rate you can from an ordinary savings account.

Short term

That is, 1–7 years. Examples – wedding, special anniversary, new carpet, work on the house, deposit for a car or a house.

A survey in June 2004 by Sainsbury – which has a bank as well as a supermarket chain – estimated that couples planning to marry would borrow £542 million in 2004 to fund what's probably the most expensive day of their lives. Much better to save, and save enough. If you are saving for something that's more than a year away, you have to decide whether to take a gamble. You can earn a bit more interest by saving in a fixed-term account – one that guarantees you a slightly better rate of return, in exchange for which you promise not to take your money out for a fixed period of a year. You can also choose two, three, four or five years. The gamble is this. Your rate of interest is fixed. If interest rates fall you will do well, because your fixed rate will look very good. But if they rise, you may find that your fixed rate looks a bit mean.

Also worth considering are National Savings & Investments products, such as their index-linked certificates. Over three or five years these promise a real return ahead of inflation and it's free of tax. See National Savings, page 157, for more details. You must be sure you can keep the money in for the full term or it will turn out to be a poor deal.

Medium term

Here I mean 7–20 years. Examples – children's savings, university fees.

For this length of time, most advisers immediately say 'stock market'. That is partly, of course, because they earn more money – indeed all their money – by recommending investments with a bit of risk to them. But it is also because most of them genuinely believe that the stock market is the best place to have your money for anything other than short-term investments. And for them, 7 to 20 years is long term. But not for me. And this is why. University starts on a set date in September when the little darlings are 18. And I haven't forgotten about the gap year. Someone has to pay for that too, don't they? When that date arrives, you need the money then. You cannot put it off for a couple of years if the markets have just had one of their periodic tumbles. Look at mortgage endowments. These were sold as cheaper and sure-fire ways to fund house purchase. They depended on experts investing your money in a mixture of shares and other things over the 25 years that the mortgage lasted. The latest estimate from the Financial Services Authority (FSA) is that these endowments will be £50 billion too little to repay the mortgages they support. So it doesn't always work. Even over 25 years. And yes, they were sold because there was lots of commission on offer.

But let's do a deal here. I say put your money into something safe like cash or government bonds. You say go for the stock market. There's a risk but there's also a chance of doing better. We do the figures and it turns out that we have to save twice as much with my scheme as yours. But it's guaranteed. We both promise this. When the kids reach 18 we will explain our decision to them then. Well, OK, they're your kids. You explain. My kids will probably be burying me by then. But just remember who you have to justify your decision to when they have to work their own way through college.

And if you do go for the stock market, see the notes below on long-term investments.

Long term

I call 'long term' more than 20 years. Examples – pension, retirement, paying off an interest-only mortgage.

If you are investing for 20 years or more, you can fairly safely think of a stock-market investment. Remember, though, that there is a chance, however small, that after charges you won't have as much at the end as you paid in.

- There is still some risk that your investment will be worth less at the end than it was at the start. (See Two or three little words, page 164.)
- Some of your money will be siphoned off each year to pay the costs

and pay commission to your adviser. (See Getting the commission back, page 163, for how to avoid this.)

■ As you approach the time you will be needing the money, you should think about moving it from the risks of the stock market to the safety of other investments or savings. (See Reaching fifty, page 86.)

■ Saving

Saving, then, is lending your money to a bank or building society and leaving it there to earn interest. The bank, of course, uses the money while it's there and the interest it pays you represents the value of the money to the bank. Or in some cases what it can get away with. If you lend £1000 to a bank for a year you can earn as little as nothing. Or as much as £60. This section looks at the basics of saving.

If you have some money in a savings account – or even in your current account – the chances are it is not earning you much. And the less it earns for you, the more it earns for the bank. So act now on lazy savings.

Tax-free savings

Tax is a drag. Literally. Whatever your savings want to race ahead and earn, they are dragged back by the Chancellor, who wants to take his share of the profit. Normally the interest earned on savings is taxed at 20 per cent. In other words, for every £100 interest, the Chancellor takes £20 and you get £80. If you have a high enough income to be a higher-rate taxpayer, then you only get £60.

And don't think higher-rate tax is only for the super-rich. Over the last ten years the number of people paying the higher-rate tax has grown by a million. Not because we are all getting richer, but because tax allowances have grown much more slowly than earnings. Higher-rate tax now starts once your income reaches £36,100 a year. Instead of paying 22 per cent of your earnings in tax, you will pay 40 per cent on income above that amount. The good news is that National Insurance is cut from 11 per cent to 1 per cent at roughly the same income level. So your overall rate of tax on earnings goes from 33 per cent to 41 per cent.

Some savings can be hidden from income tax – legally! You are allowed to put up to £3000 a year into a special kind of savings account called a cash ISA (ISA stands for individual savings account) and you pay no tax at all on the interest. Another advantage with cash ISAs is that they tend to pay some of the best rates of interest. So you can quite readily find one that pays you more than 4 per cent a year, maybe even 5 per cent or more. There are no restrictions on taking money out of a cash ISA. The one restriction is that you can only put a total of £3000 into it during the tax year. So if you save £2000 and take £1000 out, you can still put another £1000 in before the end of the tax year. But if you put in £2500 and take £1000 out, then you can only put £500 in before the end of the tax year. Just to complicate things, the government intends to cut the annual amount you can put into a cash ISA from £3000 to £1000. The change is due to happen in April 2006. But the government may relent.

Cash ISAs are ideal to save up for Christmas or a holiday, and earn tax-free interest to give your savings a bit of a boost. They are also ideal if you want to save some cash for a longer time – maybe keep £2000 in the bank for emergencies. Put it in a tax-free cash ISA and watch it grow! And because cash ISAs tend to pay the highest rates of interest, they are good for non-tax-payers too.

■ GOLDEN·RULE OF CASH SAVINGS

■ Put cash savings into a cash ISA, even for a short time

Choosing a cash ISA

Cash ISAs are simple products – you put money in, it earns interest, you pay no tax. But the financial services industry hates simplicity. It wants to offer us choice – lots of it – in the hope that some of us will make bad choices. For example, if you put £500 in a cash ISA with Barnsley Building Society in the summer of 2004 it would have earned just 0.9 per cent. But you could have got 5 per cent on that money with the best ISA providers. The simple product – a cash ISA – has been picked up, spun round and given frills, with the result that you now have more than 300 different versions to choose from.

Some pay you more if you put more in. Some pay you more if you promise to leave it there for a year or more. Some pay you less if you don't warn them you are going to take out your own money. Some want you to promise to put money in every month. And others give you more if you buy another financial product from the same company. Stick two fingers up at the lot of them. What you want is an account without any restrictions – one that will accept £1 and pay the same interest on that as £1000; one where you can take money out and put it in (subject to the legal limit of £3000 a year) when you want without giving anyone a warning. And you don't want to tie your money up for a while, thank you very much.

Independent financial advisers Chase de Vere estimate that someone who put the maximum £3000 into a cash ISA from when they started in April 1999 will have put in £18,000 by the middle of 2004 but with interest will have £20,346 in there, all earning money tax-free.

> Money won is twice as sweet as money earned
> *Eddie Felson in The Color of Money 1986*

For once the government has tried to help with keeping cash ISAs simple. It has what it calls a CAT standard. CAT stands for 'costs, access, terms', which means the costs are low, access is free and easy, and the terms are simple and fair. In other words, there are as few restrictions on your money as possible. With a CAT-marked ISA you can pay as little as £10 into the account and get your cash within seven days. But CATs are not quite the cream. You want to be able to pay in as little as £1 when you want and get your money instantly without hassle. For ordinary day-to-day savings, that should be your aim. CAT-standard cash ISAs might be called 'stakeholder' or 'Sandler' accounts from April 2005. In addition, they will have to pay a rate of interest, which is within 1 per cent of the Bank of England base rate.

There is one exception (sorry!). The very best rates of interest can be paid if you agree to leave your money in for a fixed length of time. So if you are absolutely sure that you will not need the money for one, two or three years, you can earn a bit more. That does not always happen, however. There have been times quite recently when the best instant-access account was better than the best account over a fixed term, but now the pendulum has swung the other way. And you can get an extra 0.5 or even 1 per cent by agreeing to leave your money in the ISA for a year or more.

Other savings

If you have more cash to save than you can put in a cash ISA – and remember every individual over 16 can put £3000 each tax year into it until at least April 2006 – then go for an ordinary savings or deposit account. Though it is better to find an extraordinary one! Because savings accounts are also very variable. There are hundreds of different savings accounts. And the interest rates they pay vary from more than 5 per cent a year to a tiny 0.1 per cent. In other words, if you left £1000 in there all year you would get £1 in interest – *before* tax! The average rate paid by the top ten is 4.7 per cent. The average paid by the bottom ten is 0.35 per cent. So the top ten pay nearly 14 times as much interest as the bottom ten.

Things to avoid

Give the following a wide berth!

Temporary rates We are in the era of the Best Buy table. Several commercial companies offer these – you'll find them in newspapers and hear about them on radio programmes. Companies bust a gut to get their product into the best buys and, of course, find all sorts of ways of getting in there. The most popular is the bonus rate. They offer you a bonus of 0.5 per cent or so on your savings *but it only lasts six months*. Out of the top six instant-access accounts as I write, four offer a temporary bonus rate. When that runs out, these accounts will drop straight out of the top ten. For example, at the time of writing Northern Rock offers 5.01 per cent on your savings, putting it second in the best-buy tables. But that rate falls to 4.3 per cent after six months. That puts it at 22nd place in the best buys! So don't be fooled by bonus rates.

Notice accounts These are the opposite of instant access. You have to give notice before you can get your own money out. But the rates you get are generally no better than the rates you get from the best instant-access accounts. Avoid them. If you can afford to tie your money up, then consider a fixed-rate bond.

Minimum deposit Some accounts make you save a certain amount before giving you the best deals. But the best rates are still to be found on accounts that pay the full rate on the first pound. So avoid accounts that make you save more than you might want to.

Things to watch for

Make sure you're well informed about the following.

Monthly interest Some accounts pay interest monthly, others annually. But they should all quote interest as an AER (annual equivalent rate) and that's the thing you should use to compare them. Monthly interest is useful for people who want an income from their savings. But you need a lot of savings to get a significant monthly income. For example, if you have £20,000 savings, you could get around £80 a month income – £64 after tax. It can also be useful if you are saving up for something and want the interest to boost what you've saved before a year is up.

Withdrawals Some accounts limit the amount of money you can withdraw or the number of withdrawals you make.

Branch, post or internet Some accounts are internet only, others are post or telephone only. Only rarely can best-buy accounts be operated through a branch.

> **In almost every case the best things to look for in a savings account are instant access, no restrictions and an account that pays in full on £1. Go for the highest rate of interest.**

National Savings

Experts disagree about whether the products from National Savings & Investments are savings or investments. You can argue it both ways. Certainly NS&I has some pure savings accounts; some of the others seem more like investments. But in my book (especially this one) they are all savings products. You can debate whether the money you invest remains yours or is technically the government's, but the returns – including the return of your money in full – are guaranteed by the state. And you can't get safer than that.

So I count NS&I products as savings. Despite their name. Confusing names and twisted English are all part of the wonderful world of personal finance. Even when it comes to the government.

You pay a price for the cast-iron certainty of National Savings. You can always do slightly better than NS&I with a bank or building society savings account. But people like the guarantee and the products are very popular. Unfortunately, they're not always that simple.

One of the best NS&I deals is its index-linked savings certificates – you won't get an investment like this anywhere else. You invest any amount from £100 to £15,000. You must keep it there for three or five years. At the end of that time you get your money back plus interest equal to the rate of inflation, plus 1.25 per cent a year if you invest for three years, or 1.35 per cent a year for the five-year investment. And it's all tax-free. So your savings stay ahead of inflation and escape the tax-man.

There are lots of other NS&I products and you can find out more on its website – see Follow-up at the end of the book.

■ Investing

Some people see investing as the big brother of saving. I prefer to see it as the crafty cousin. Remember, when you invest, *the money stops being yours.* So you have to trust the person or company whose financial product you have bought. Think of it like Mr Oldenshaw's chair. Will it grow in value? How do you know? Will anyone want to buy it? What are the costs of selling it? While you are sitting on it, will one leg break off?

Shares

For the last 50 years, shares have been at the heart of the pensions and investments of most people in the UK. And don't think, 'He doesn't mean me.' I do. If you pay into a pension, have a mortgage endowment, put some money into a unit trust, have a with-profits policy, or a life insurance product that pays out before you die, then you are a part owner of some shares.

A 'share' is just what it says – a share of a company. It is, of course, a very small share. One of Britain's biggest companies is the telecoms giant

Vodafone. There are about 68 billion shares in Vodafone. So if you have one share you own one sixty-eight-billionth of the company. Each share is worth about £1.30, making the whole company worth about £88 billion.

If you own a share you can make money in two ways:

- The company can pay you some of the profit it makes. That is called a dividend and it represents your return on the money you've invested.
- The value of the shares will go up and down, but overall you hope the value will rise. So that if you buy £500 worth of shares, you hope in a few years' time you'll be able to sell them for more than £500.

Let's see how that might work with Vodafone. Measuring the profit of a large and complex thing like a company is very difficult, especially when it operates in several countries and is often in the middle of buying and selling other companies. So there are several ways of doing it. Using one method, Vodafone made £10 billion profit in 2003–2004. In other words, what it took from its customers was £10 billion more than it spent on its staff and running the network. If that £10 billion was shared equally between all its shareholders – remember, there are 68 billion of them – they would get about 14p for each share they owned. In fact, Vodafone had many other things to do with its money, such as investing in a new network and paying off some of its huge debts. So most of the profits were kept for those things and the company paid its investors just 2p for each share they held. A share is currently worth around £1.30. So if you invested in Vodafone you would get a return of just 2p for each £1.30 you invested, which is about 1.5 per cent – even worse than the banks will pay.

But there is a second part to investing. Most people expect to make a profit on their shares: they expect the price of the shares to go up over the period they hold them. Like the antique chair, you buy at one price and sell at a higher price. If you're lucky. Vodafone shares were worth just 80p each on 3 July 2002. Today as I write, about two years later, they are worth £1.30. So if you bought £500 of Vodafone shares in July 2002 and sold them two years later you would have got £812, a profit of £312. Even better than Mr Oldenshaw's chair. But July 2002 was the low point for Vodafone. A year earlier the shares cost £1.68 each. And a year before that they cost about £3. In fact, they peaked at £3.83 on 10 March 2000. So if you bought then, your investment is now worth less than half what you paid for it. A thumping great loss. Or what some City optimists might call a negative profit. And this is the problem with shares as an investment. They can make you a lot of money. But they can also cost you a great deal.

The price of a share in a particular company depends on lots of things. Some of them make sense. If a company is making strong profits then its shares should be more valuable than those of a company that's making a loss. The people who run it are also important. Do the directors do their job well? Have they got a clear vision of the future? On the negative side, if a company seems to be heading for bankruptcy, then its shares will quickly become valueless. Technically, the price of the shares represents the value now of the expectation of its profits in the future. The quality of the managers, the demand for the products the company makes and its vision of the future will all help put a price on its shares.

But the price is also affected by things that are nothing to do with the business at all. If investors believe that the price of shares in a company will rise, they can buy for that reason alone, hoping to make a quick profit. That happens, for example, when one company tries to take over another – shares in the target company rise in the belief that the price will go up as the predator tries to convince shareholders to sell. When a very rich man called Philip Green revealed he wanted to buy Marks & Spencer in May 2004, the price of its shares rose by almost £1 each overnight.

It's not just takeovers that lead to expectations of share price rises. In the late 1990s people went mad over high-technology companies, especially those based around providing services over the internet. People believed they were the next big thing and the price of their shares could only rise. And so they bought them. And as demand grew so did the price. Which was strange. Because most of the high-tech companies lost money every year, had no prospect of making a profit and owed huge debts. In March 2000 investors paused for a reality check. Shares in high-tech companies fell out of favour and the price plummeted, taking a lot of other companies down too. The market has still not recovered from that crash.

Just as shares can go up because everyone expects the value to rise, so the price can fall because people anticipate it falling. Everyone tries to sell before it's too late, driving the price down further. Investors are said to have 'lost confidence' in the company.

So if it is all so uncertain, why does just about every financial adviser recommend that any money we have to invest should be put into shares? One reason is that while investing in one company is risky, investing in a whole range of shares is less so. As one company's shares go down, so others will go up. So when you invest in shares you seldom buy and sell shares in one or two companies yourself. Instead you put your money into a fund which owns shares in lots of companies. In this way you smooth out the ups and downs that affect individual companies.

Indeed, the financial health of the nation's businesses is normally measured by the rise and fall of the average share price of the biggest 100 companies in the UK. The price is measured by the FTSE100 index, which you will hear quoted in just about every news bulletin on television and radio. 'In the City the FTSE is up eight points at forty-four fifteen.' To most people that's pretty meaningless. So here's a quick explanation. The index started at 1000 in February 1984. As share prices rise and fall, so the index changes. If the index was 2000 it would mean that shares in the biggest 100 companies were worth twice as much as they were when the index began. When it reaches 4500 they will be worth four and a half times as much. When broadcasters say it's 'forty-four fifteen', they really mean 'four thousand four hundred and fifteen'. Now, at last, you know what that nonsense is all about!

And it is indexes like this which show that, over the years, investments in shares make more money than investments in just about anything else. Researchers have gone back more than a century to 1900, and when investments are compared over this period, money invested in shares is shown to grow more than money saved in bank accounts or invested in safe things like government bonds.

This is particularly true over the last quarter of the last century. From 1975 to 1999 the price of shares in UK companies rose every single year except three – and on those three occasions prices rose strongly the following year. Over that time share prices rose on average by 12.8 per cent a year. That was an amazing return on your money. It seemed like a one-way bet. A whole generation of financial advisers had never seen share prices do anything but go up year after year after year. The occasional stumble was nothing more than a temporary glitch. So it is not surprising that they told everyone to put their money in the stock market.

But then came 2000. Prices fell. And in 2001 they fell again, by more. And in 2002 they fell again, by more still. Between their peak on 31 December 1999 and their low point in March 2003, share prices fell by more than half. Someone investing in June 1995 and taking the money out nearly eight years later in March 2003 would have found it had not grown by one penny. So the stock market is not a sure-fire bet, even if we spread our investment over all the bigger companies.

Back to the question, Why do advisers keep recommending that we put money in shares? The first reason is that most of them have never known anything else. Secondly, historically over the long term it has been good advice. And thirdly, they get paid more commission for recommending stock market-based investments.

Commission is at the heart of the financial services industry. Of course, all businesses that depend on sales pay their staff commission. The more they sell, the more they make. But financial products are different from other things we might buy, such as a suit or a washing machine, because:

- They are much more expensive.
- They are much less easy to understand.
- It is much harder to see if anything goes wrong.
- It is much more difficult to get your money back.

Since the end of 2004, people selling financial services have had to tell us more clearly how much commission they are being paid. For example, if you invest in a unit trust, out of the charges you pay the adviser will get around 4 per cent of the money invested and then 0.5 per cent a year of the value of the investment. So if you invest a lump sum of £10,000, the adviser will get £400 to start and then £50 a year for as long as you keep the investment going. If the investment grows, then this annual commission will grow as well. But these amounts are tiny compared with the commission paid on products where you commit yourself to saving regularly.

For example, with some personal pensions, as much as 80 per cent of the first year's premiums can be paid in commission to the person who sold it to you. In addition, he or she will get an annual payment – as much as 0.5 or even 1 per cent of the value of your pension fund. Instead of going to your pension for the future, it goes to pay the adviser's salary. Even with stake-holder pensions, which should be cheaper, probably the first four months' contributions you pay don't go into the fund at all – instead they go to your adviser. And you will be paying perhaps £3 of every £1000 in your pension fund to your adviser every year until you retire.

These annual commissions – also called renewal or trail commission – are supposed to encourage your sales rep to keep in touch and review your finances. To act in other words like a real financial adviser – the title most of them adopt but few really fulfil. Too many of them simply take the money and run. The only time you are likely to hear from them is when they want to sell you something else.

Getting the commission back

A stockbroker is someone who invests your money until it is all gone.

Anon

Commission is a pain. You cannot avoid it by buying direct from the insurance company or bank. Commission is so rooted in the structure of the financial services industry that if you do buy direct, the bank or insurer just keeps the commission itself. However, a growing number of financial advisers will claim the commission and then give it, or some of it, back to you. They are called discount brokers. They work like this. The commission is still paid. Like the tide, you cannot stop it; you just have to manage it. But the adviser gives almost all of it back to you. They can afford to do that because they do not give you advice, they just do what you ask. You decide what you need and what to buy and they take no responsibility for it. You can invest in unit trusts, OEICs, pensions, bonds and buy them through an investment ISA if you want. Normally these discount brokers operate through the internet, and although they do not give face-to-face advice, their websites will give you guidance about risk and what you should invest in. But beware – it may not always be very good advice.

Similar to discount brokers are fund supermarkets. But they tend to charge more and let you have a more limited range of products.

Two or three little words

If you ask your financial adviser about stock-market investments, he or she will always mention two little words. One is risk. The other is long term. (OK, long term is two words by itself.) Let's look at these two (three) little words.

Risk You've got to take a risk to get the reward – that's what they will say. They will also ask you what your attitude to risk is, or try to devise what they call a 'risk profile'. But the way they talk about it you would think it was a one-way bet. You take something called a 'risk' and you will get a reward. But, of course, risk does not mean that. Risk means you can lose money as well as make it. Strangely, the downside is never mentioned much. So when you are asked about your attitude to risk, think to yourself: 'I've got £1000. I give it to this person and in a year's time I've only got £600. How will I feel?'

> **A. Terrible** – I worked hard for that money and I did not want it lost to someone else, either through commission or poor investment.
>
> **B. A bit upset** – I was told it was a risk but I did not really expect to lose money. You don't, do you?
>
> **C. Quite happy** – I knew I could lose it but I also knew there was a chance I could make more than I could in a savings account. It was a bet. I lost. Some you win, some you lose.

If you answered C, you are a true stock-market investor. But read about 'long term' opposite before putting your hard-earned into shares.

If you answered A, you should put your money in the best savings account you can find and do not go near a financial adviser.

You put B? You still haven't understood what risk means. Either read what I say about risk again, or say this out loud: RISK MEANS I COULD LOSE MY MONEY. Twenty times.

Long term The other mantra you will hear is 'stock-market investments are for the long term', usually followed by 'about five years or more'. Wrong. If you picked any period of five years in the last hundred and you spread your money across all the companies listed on the London stock market, you would have one chance in three of ending up no better off at the end. Of course, you would have two chances in three of making money – sometimes not very much, sometimes a lot. But a one in three chance of losing money is not very good.

So maybe it's ten years? No. After ten years, the odds lengthen to about one chance in four of ending up no better off.

Fifteen? Funnily enough, 15 years is no better than ten.

So how long is long term? Well, 100 is a good number. Over the last 100 years, stock market-based investments have done better than investments in other things. Trouble is, humans don't have 100 years to wait. Fortunately, 25 years is not much worse. But much less than 25 and there's a real risk you will end up worse off – or at least no better off – than when you started. But don't take my word for it. Here is the view of the financial regulator, the Financial Services Authority. In June 2003 I interviewed Norman Digance, then its General Manager of Investment Business, about investment returns. The FSA had been looking at what financial companies could say about the money your investments would make. I asked him on BBC Radio 4: 'How long is long term?'

> DIGANCE: Well, basically long term – I mean in our – in our words is basically 20 to 25 years.
>
> LEWIS: So you're saying now that the FSA's view of what is a long-term investment is 20 to 25 years?
>
> DIGANCE: Yes, there's nothing new about that.

So there it is. And when a financial adviser tells you that long term means 'at least five years and perhaps ten', remind them of what the regulator says. And perhaps ask if he or she knows how many times investments have gone down, rather than up, over a five-year period. You now know it's one out of three. I bet they won't. And you might add that the FSA in a recent report said: 'Over an even shorter time frame [than five years], the equity market is more like a game of chance than an investment.'

Think before investing

If I have not put you off investing for ever, one more warning. Before you think about investing money, check two things. First, look at your debts. If you still have some, the best thing to do with any spare money you have – whether in the bank or more money you have each month than you spend – is to use it to pay that debt off. You will never make more by investing £1000 than the money you are being charged to borrow it. So pay off your credit card debt, get rid of the overdraft and see if you can pay off any bank loans early without being charged heavy penalties. Even using it to pay a bit off your mortgage or student loan can be a better use for your money than investing it. Second, make sure you do have some money in cash – emergency money, run-away money, treats money.

Once you have done those two things, you might think about investing. So now it's time for not just a Golden Rule, but a Golden and Sparkly Rule.

▤ GOLDEN AND SPARKLY RULE OF INVESTING

■ Don't put all your eggs in one basket

Now, that's not very original, I know. And I can't even amuse you by telling you where it came from. No one seems to know. It's a proverb certainly dating back at least to the middle of the 17th century. Perhaps Jack was actually coming back from the chicken house when he and Jill ran up the hill. He insisted he had all the eggs in his basket because he was the boy and the oldest. So they all got broken. Jill sensibly left her basket at the bottom of the hill before she went running up. But it was empty. If they had shared them then at least some of the eggs would have been saved. Enough for an omelette anyway. Sadly, Seventeenth-century Proverbs is not a course of study normally taken by financial advisers.

But the thing about investing is that there is *always* a risk. So if all your eggs – and it applies particularly to nest eggs – are in one wobbly basket, they are all at the same risk of that big wobble. But if some are in a wobbly basket, others in a basket that's a bit weak at the seams, and yet more in one made of very thin cane, the chance of seams and cane breaking and wobble happening all at the same time is much less than that of just one of them happening. It's called spreading the risk.

Nowadays many of the better IFAs will talk to you grandly about 'asset allocation' and putting your money into a mixture or balance of 'asset classes'. That's posh talk for spreading the risk. And, yes, not putting all your eggs, etc. But it's good advice none the less.

Anyway, pressing on. Whatever sort of investment you consider there are certain key questions to ask.

Risk How safe is your money? What's the worst that could happen?
Return What gain can you expect? Will you get an income? Or will your investment grow in value? What guarantees are there of income or capital growth?
Access How easy is it to get your money out? Will you have to sell your investment? Will there be anyone to buy it? Do you have to give notice? Are there penalties to pay? What will be the cost of selling?
Charges How much of your money will be drained away in charges? What will those charges buy for you? What will be the long-term effect?

You should also check that any company you are dealing with is registered in the UK and that there is a compensation scheme in place. And check that the way the investment and its returns are taxed suits you. There is no point in using a tax-free investment if you don't pay tax.

Safer investments

We'll get to stock-market investing later. First, here are some safer forms of investing.

Government stock (also called gilts) Probably the only safe way of investing. You buy a £100 certificate from the government and it guarantees to pay you a fixed rate of interest twice a year until a certain date. At that date, the government gives you back £100 – guaranteed. Short of the collapse of the world as we know it, gilts are 100 per cent safe. You are lending money to the government.

You can buy gilts direct from the government – through a place called the Debt Management Office – or you can buy them through dealers (they are called 'brokers', but that's just a posh name for dealers). There are low charges to pay. Gilts can seem complicated. And they are not very popular with financial advisers because they get no commission for recommending them. But if you want a safe guaranteed investment for a few years, then gilts are great. You can even get them linked to the rate of inflation. The income they pay you is taxable. Contact the Bank of England for an application form (see Follow-up, page 205).

> High interest is another name for bad security.
>
> *Duke of Wellington*

Corporate bonds are similar to gilts, but they don't come with a government guarantee. You lend the company money and it promises to pay you interest on your money and repay it in full at the end of a fixed period. But the promise is only as good as the company. If it gets into financial difficulties, it may not be able to pay you your money. It may even go bust. If so, you get paid ahead of other people who are owed money, but you might still lose all or most of your investment. Corporate bonds have a star rating. The best are AAA (almost certainly won't go bust), down through AA, A, B and BB to reach BBB, where there is a fair risk you will not get your money back. Why, you may ask, would anyone invest in a BBB bond? The return is higher, about 3 or 4 per cent more than AAA bonds. But you may not get it. We are back to gambling your capital on getting a higher return.

Stock-market investments
So finally we come to putting your money on the roulette wheel that is called the stock market. Let me just remind you of what this means.

Your money is at risk Remember the old saying – shares can go down as well as plummet. With care you can minimize the risk of losing your money, but any stock market-based investment can result in your getting back less than you put in.

It's not your money If you have used your money to buy shares in companies, you own shares, not money. And, just like Mr Oldenshaw's chair, when you want money you must find someone to buy these shares and take the price you are offered. The buying price is always less than the selling price, so you start with a loss. And there will be fees and tax to pay on the deal.

Drained off Not all your money will have been invested. You will probably pay upfront charges – in other words, you give someone £100 to invest and they keep £5 and invest £95. Then each year they will drain off some of your money. Normally at least 1 per cent, and sometimes 2 per cent or even more.

> Beware of small expenses; a small leak will sink a great ship.
>
> *Benjamin Franklin*

Time is not on your side Shares need a long time to be anything like a sure bet. So you have to be sure you really will not need the money in the short term. You may need it to pay a debt, deal with an emergency, help with university fees or pay a tax bill. And when that need comes along, that might be just the wrong time to sell.

Logic doesn't work The value of shares often moves for apparently irrational reasons. Although we are all told to invest in shares for the long term, the price of shares is determined almost entirely by the short-term buying and selling done by dealers. They may own the shares for a few days, even as little as an hour. Indeed they may never own them at all, just buying and selling promises to buy or sell them later.

Spreading the risk

> There is some ill a-brewing towards my rest,
> For I did dream of money-bags to-night.
>
> *Shylock, Merchant of Venice II v 17*

Shares used to be for the rich. Not any more. The financial services industry has dreamed up products to let anyone put their money at risk on the stock market. These products do two things.

- They protect you from some of the risk.
- They protect the industry from all of the risk – they make money whether shares go down or up.

Instead of buying shares in one company, you buy a share in a fund that uses the money from thousands of investors to buy a whole range of shares. Some shares will fall, but others will rise and overall the value of the fund will rise. That's the theory.

There are two basic sorts of fund: managed and tracker funds. Managed funds, as their name suggests, are managed by experts who draw on a large research department to study the whole market, visit major companies to assess how they are being run, and take account of economic and other factors to decide where the best place is to invest your money. They then buy shares in those companies and you hope their judgement is right.

Tracker funds simply rely on the fact that overall the average price of all shares tends to rise over time. So, instead of doing all that expensive work and study, they simply spread your money across the shares in all the companies that have them. In that way they will follow the index of the whole market up – and, of course, down. They are called tracker funds because they follow, or track, the market index.

Trackers have two big advantages. First, they are cheaper to run. They need a small number of modestly paid people to run the computer system and buy and sell the shares as the computer determines. This should be passed on to you in lower charges. In other words, the fund administrators take less of your money each year. Second, in the long term they do better than managed funds. Of course, in any one or two years, some managed funds will do better than a fund that tracks the market. That's easy to see at the end of the year, but research shows it is impossible to predict at the start of the year. A good fund one year will not necessarily be a good fund the next year. One thing does pass on from year to year. Bad funds tend to stay bad funds. A dog is always a dog. But a star rises and falls. There is no 'persistency', as it is called. That's why there are now strict controls by the FSA on the 'past performance' figures that can be used in adverts. And since these controls came in, you almost never see such performance figures quoted.

Some people will tell you that although particular funds cannot be relied on, the people who manage them can. So if you move your money from one fund to another as the manager moves – and gets paid loads more – then you can hitch your investment wagon to a star. Not any more. Research published in July 2004 showed that out of 175 fund managers with a five-year track record, only 11, that is 6 per cent, managed to do better than the market average every year for five years. And there's no evidence that they will continue to do better in the future. So picking the ones who will do well over the next five years – which is what matters – is an impossible task.

Trackers follow particular markets – such as the FTSE All Share index of the London Stock Exchange or the Nikkei index in Tokyo. Or they may follow an index of high-tech companies. If you believe that shares rise overall and you have money for the long term, then a tracker fund – sometimes called a 'passive' fund – that follows the index of all shares in London is the best idea.

If you are feeling a bit more adventurous, you can buy an alternative to a tracker called an exchange traded fund (ETF). These are shares (one branded by Barclays is called iShares), and they are a cheaper way to link your fortunes to a particular market, part of the world or type of industry. The Barclays FTSE iShare is the most popular but there are ETFs that track almost any market in the world – from Japan to Switzerland. Alternatively, you can invest in what professionals call a sector, such as oil and gas, telecoms, small companies. Charges are lower than unit trusts with no initial charge and only 0.5 per cent a year taken from your money to run the scheme. That's a very small hole in your investment bucket, and some ETFs charge even less. You can put ETFs into an investment ISA if you want, though unless you pay higher-rate tax or expect to pay capital gains tax, there is no point. You need to buy them through a broker. (See Getting the commission back on page 163.)

The main risk with ETFs is that you can make the wrong choices. Just because oil or gas or the Japanese stock market have done well in the last year or so doesn't mean they will do well next year. But even if you just want to hitch your fortunes to the wagon of the FTSE 100 index, iShares are a cheap way to do it.

Managed funds are more complicated. You could be offered funds invested in Asia and China, in Japan, in Global Growth, in Special Situations,

Emerging Markets or Global Optimal Thirds. No, I don't know what that means either. Others specialize in smaller companies or organizations dealing in property or precious metals. If you see words like 'growth', 'income', 'cautious', 'escalator', 'safety', these are not promises or descriptions of how your investment will do. The companies will tell you they express the 'hopes' or 'aspirations' of the fund. But they are simply words used as marketing tools.

The other big disadvantage with managed funds is that they cost a lot more to run and you pay for that through the annual charges. Whereas a tracker will charge you around 1 per cent a year – some a bit more, some a bit less – a managed fund may charge you 2 or 2.5 per cent a year and will often charge you 5 per cent of your money just to set it up. Given that overall they do not do any better than trackers, they are a waste of money.

Sandler and stakeholder

A few years ago the government got very concerned about why people weren't saving enough. It decided that among the influencing factors was the complexity and expense of financial products. It asked a man called Ron Sandler to look at these problems and he recommended that financial companies should be encouraged to produce a range of savings products that would be simple to understand, with low costs and limited risk.

These 'Sandler' products come on the market in April 2005. Some of them are also called 'stakeholder' products, because the government thought it would help people understand them if they had two names and neither of them meant anything. These Sandler or stakeholder products will be sold by unqualified advisers, who also start work from April 2005 (see table page 187).

There will be a medium-term investment (which in this context the government says is five to ten years) that puts a maximum of 60 per cent of your money at risk on the stock market. (The rest is in safer things like bonds.) The investment will come in two forms – one where the ups and downs of the stock market are 'smoothed', and one where they are not. The charges will be up to 1.7 per cent a year for the 'smoothed' version and 1.5 per cent a year for the other.

Pensions were the first product to get the stakeholder label. Stakeholder pensions began in April 1999. Charges were restricted to 1 per cent a year.

But they are going to be relaunched in April 2005 as a Sandler product and will be allowed to charge more – up to 1.5 per cent a year. For some reason the government expects these higher charges to encourage more people to save.

There will also be a simple savings account, similar to the cash ISA (see Tax-free savings, page 153). In fact, it may replace it. At the time of writing, however, there are no details yet on how much can be saved in it each year or what the tax treatment will be.

Ethics

If, like many financial advisers, you think ethics is a county to the east of London, then skip the next paragraph. But if you care what companies do with your money, read on. More and more people are concerned that the money they invest is put to good use. Or, at least, not put to bad use. Perhaps you would be unhappy if you thought your money was being used to buy shares in companies that make armaments or tobacco or alcohol. Some people object to drug or oil companies. Others don't want to be involved in gambling, farming or pornography, or anything that conflicts with their religious views. Some Muslims, for example, will not invest in many banks or insurance companies because they believe lending money at interest is wrong. Everyone has their own list of what they do or don't like in the business world.

Other people see ethical investing as a more positive thing – they want their money to be used by firms that positively try to put something back in the environment. They want to invest in green energy – wind farms and the like – or companies that behave in a socially responsible way. There are a few – a very few – people who work in the financial services industry who share these concerns and will try to help you invest in a green way. Although a MORI poll found 65 per cent of people would like to know that their money was being used for good, financial advisers claim that barely 1 in 20 of their customers ever mentions this. If you want to find out more about ethical investments, contact the Social Investment Forum (see Follow-up, page 205). It claims that investments in ethical funds are overall no worse and no better than ones in non-ethical funds. Some are good, some are bad.

Buying a fund

There are many funds to choose from. Here are your main options.

Unit trusts This is the simplest way to buy into a managed or tracker fund. The trust owns the shares and you buy a small share of that fund so that your money is spread across all the shares it has bought. Your bit is measured in the number of units you buy in the trust. You can buy and sell your units, and you will be told each year how many units you have and what they are worth.

Investment trusts Despite their name, these are companies that invest in the shares of other companies. You buy a share in the investment trust company, which of course you can sell when you want to realize your cash. Because investment trusts are companies they can borrow money and can take more risks than unit trusts, which means the value of your share is likely to go up and down more than the units in a trust. Investment trusts are not regulated by the FSA.

Open-Ended Investment Companies or OEICs Yes, it is pronounced oiks! These are a bit like unit trusts and bit like investment trusts, and a kind of collective investment that's common in other European countries. They are regulated by the FSA.

Note: Although most of these funds invest your money (mainly) on the stock market, you can find safer ones that invest some or all of the money they handle in corporate bonds or gilts, or even cash. These funds will be safer in the sense that you are less likely to lose your money. But beware. Even funds that are invested in the safest of safe things will take charges off you.

With profits These are now considered a bit old-fashioned, and, of course, the term 'with profits' is meaningless. After several years of poor performance and cuts in returns, many wits have said they would be better called 'with losses'. A with-profits fund is run by an insurance company and invested in a mixture of shares, bonds, property, cash and other things. The insurance company experts decide on the balance of these investments and generally tell you, the investor, very little about it.

Each year the insurance company gives you what it calls a 'bonus', which is actually the return on your investment. And at the end of the investment it gives you a final 'bonus', which represents the difference between what they have given you year by year and how much your money has actually grown. Nowadays the latter may well be zero or negative. With-profits funds used to be the cautious and sensible investment that no adviser could do wrong by recommending – and they got very good commission for selling them. So it was win–win. They won. The insurance company won. And the punter took the risk. And often lost. Nowadays they are best avoided unless:

- you trust insurance companies completely,
- you don't want to know or understand what is going on with your money.

Equity (or investment) ISAs We came across cash ISAs earlier and cash ISAs are a good thing. You save money. You get interest. You pay no tax. But there is another sort of ISA (individual savings account), which is *not* a savings account at all. It is a way of investing in a unit trust or such like, but again you pay no tax. Or at least not much. These are normally called equity ISAs, and – you guessed it – that's a misleading name. Sometimes they are invested in 'equities' (the posh word for shares), but they can also be invested in bonds, property or even cash (not your cash, someone else's). So I prefer the term 'investment ISAs'. Returns on money invested through an ISA are supposed to be tax-free. That's the point of them. But unless you pay higher-rate tax, there's no tax advantage in an investment ISA that's invested in shares. You can put up to £3000 a year in an investment ISA. Alternatively, if you don't put any money into a cash ISA in the tax year, you can invest up to £7000 in an investment ISA. I do not recommend that. Baskets, eggs and so on.

You may also be offered other investments that seem to promise exceptional returns at low risk. Nothing can do this. Even if they are legal, their main purpose will be to make money for the company that makes them and the adviser who sells them. If you do not understand it, do not put your money in it. There may be none of it left in a year or two.

▣ GOLDEN RULE OF NOT BEING STUFFED

■ If it seems too good to be true, it probably is

▣ Pensions

Sort out your debts. Put a bit of money in an instant-access account. Then sort out your pension. It may seem a long way off but retirement is just a few wrinkles away. People are not born old. It creeps up on you. And the sooner you can put some money into very long-term savings for your pension, the better. Because retirement is by definition a long way from youth, there are even more uncertainties about it than there are about other things. But we are all living longer and scientists say that lifetimes will continue to get longer. So we are all going to have to take care of ourselves in our old age.

Why bother?

What will you live on when you retire? And a shrug does *not* count as an answer! Look at the arithmetic. Do you earn £20,500 a year? If so you are bang in the middle of full-time earners. Half earn more than that, half earn less. What would you like to retire on? Half that? Life would be tough but let's see what that means. If you retire at 65 – there is little hope of it being any earlier, and it may well be later – then you will have about 16 years' retirement if you're a bloke and 19 years if you're a woman. Life expectancy figures have always been underestimates, so let's fix on 20 years. That means you would need around £200,000 to fund your retirement if you just retired and spent it. Of course, you don't know how long you will live so the sensible thing to do is to buy what is called an annuity – a guaranteed pension for life – which goes up with inflation every year. To get £10,250 a year at 65 infla-tion-proofed would cost you just over £200,000. The average amount in a pension fund today is around £25,000. That will buy you a pension at 65 of around £1250 a year – £24 a week. So you have a lot of saving to do. Or live in penury. That's why bother.

But what about the state pension? In the middle of the 1980s a very important decision was made by the Thatcher government: the state pension would be abandoned. And everyone would be expected to save for their own retirement. Of course, the state pension would not be scrapped. That was too radical even for Margaret Thatcher. But its roots would be bound and its branches chopped to leave a bonsai pension. And you don't get much fruit – or indeed much shade – from that, although it still needs an army of civil-service gardeners to look after it.

The result is that after a lifetime's work and contributions, the full state pension for most people is just £79.60 a week – £4139 a year. And if anyone reading this can live on that they are very frugal indeed. Most people in full-time work would earn that much working one day a week. Even someone on the minimum wage would earn the state pension in just two days.

Fortunately there is a back-up in the form of a second pension from the state that is related to your earnings. This is called the State Second Pension, and was formerly known as SERPS. At the moment the maximum amount it provides is £140 a week, or more than £7000 a year, though most people get far less. The State Second Pension has three advantages over a pension you might save up for yourself.

- It is fully index-linked
- Your spouse will get half of it when you die
- It is guaranteed by the state

Everyone pays into the State Second Pension automatically, unless they choose to 'opt out'. You normally have to opt out if you pay into a pension scheme run by your employer. And you will be encouraged to opt out by your financial adviser if you pay into a personal pension.

GOLDEN RULE OF STATE PENSIONS

- Never opt out of the State Second Pension if you have the choice

If you do opt out of the State Second Pension, the government will either charge you and your employer less National Insurance, or it will charge you the same and hand over part of the contributions to your pension provider. And it will add on tax relief and, in some circumstances, an age-related bonus to reflect what it saves from not having to pay you a State Second Pension. But all that is not enough to make it worth opting out. Remember the Golden – and Sparkly – Rule of Investment? On page 166? Don't put all your eggs in one basket? The same is true of pensions. Don't put all your faith in your employer's pension, your own personal pension or the state pension. Have something in all three.

Employer's pensions

A pension run by your employer can be called an occupational pension, because it is run as part of your occupation, or it can be called a company scheme, though many people do not work for a company as such. It's all part of the great word chase that confuses us all.

And now we have sorted that out, there are two completely different sorts of pension scheme run by employers for their staff.

Salary-related pensions

The best sort promises you a pension that's a fraction of your salary for each year you pay into the scheme. Normally you get one-eightieth for each year you're in. So after 40 years you get forty-eightieths, which is half your salary. In addition, you can get a lump sum of three times your pension.

The salary figure that's used to calculate your pension is usually the average of your last three years' pay. So late promotion boosts your pension! But some schemes are moving towards using what they call a 'career average' salary – in other words, the average pay you got throughout your time in the scheme. Even though the calculation of your average pay takes inflation into account, that will usually give a lower pension. Because for most people their pay goes up during their working life. The schemes also provide life insurance, a pension for your widow or widower, and some sort of inflation-proofing for the pension you get.

A salary-related pension is common in the public sector such as the NHS, the teaching profession, the civil service and so on, where it is often called 'superannuation'. It is also found in a number of the biggest companies. But many are now closing these schemes to new members, afraid of the cost and

the long-term commitment they entail. In the USA at least two major companies have gone bust as a result of the cost of their pension schemes.

Salary-related pension schemes can also be called defined benefit –
sometimes abbreviated to DB – schemes, because it is the amount of the benefit, or pension, that is defined, and sufficient contributions have to be paid
in by you and your employer to sustain them.

If your employer runs a salary-related scheme, *join it*. You will not get a
better deal anywhere. Don't worry if you think you may not be with that
employer for 40 years. If you move jobs, you can either leave the pension
there and claim what you have earned when you retire, or you can take the
value of it and move it to another scheme in the future. This is particularly
true in the public sector, where you can move from job to job but keep the
same or a very similar pension throughout. And, of course, an eye will blink,
time will pass, and 40 years from now you just might be in the same job.
There is one small risk with these pensions. If your employer goes bust then it
cannot guarantee that there's enough in the pension fund to pay the pensions promised. This danger should be partly solved from April 2006 when a
new Pension Protection Fund begins. But there is a small risk with any company that the pension you expect will not in fact be paid in full.

In many salary-related schemes, especially in the public sector, you can
buy back some of the years you may have missed, or even years before you
worked there. These are good value. Each year you buy boosts your pension
by a year (normally one-eightieth of your final pay). And it boosts the lump
sum you can have, too. They are called 'added years'. Don't confuse them
with AVCs (see below).

People in salary-related schemes are normally opted out of the State
Second Pension and have no choice about opting back in.

Money purchase schemes

The other sort of employer's pension is not nearly as good. It simply saves up
all the contributions paid by you and your employer and puts them into a
pension fund. The money is invested and when you retire you are given the
value of your share of the fund. You then have to use that money to buy a
pension – an income for life – from an insurance company. As a rough guide,

at the time of writing, if your fund is £100,000, a woman of 65 would get an index-linked pension of about £5000 a year. A man would get £135 or so more, because he can expect to live a shorter time than a woman.

You can take up to a quarter of the fund as a tax-free lump sum, but of course that will reduce the pension you are paid. There are two reasons why money purchase schemes are worse than salary-related schemes.

There are no guarantees The pension you get depends on how much is paid in, how much the pension fund grows, and how much pension your fund will buy when you retire.

The employer pays in less They don't have to, of course, but typically the money going into a money purchase scheme is barely half that going into a final salary scheme. Inevitably this means that the pension you get will be less than half as big – and usually much less than that.

These schemes are also known as 'defined contribution' (DC) schemes because it's the amount of the contribution that is defined, not the benefits you get at the end. And because the financial services industry loves a new name, especially a meaningless acronym.

Although these schemes are not as good as a final salary scheme, if your employer is putting money in too, then it's foolish not to join. You are giving up free money.

People in money purchase schemes may or may not be opted out of the State Second Pension. If you are opted out, you do not normally have a choice about opting back in as an individual. But you could lobby your employer to ask if it is possible.

Boosting your pension

However much you save into a pension, it will not normally be enough. Recent estimates suggest that someone aged 25 should save 18 per cent of their pay all their working life if they hope to have a pension of two-thirds of their salary. At 35, that percentage goes up to around a quarter of your pay, and don't even ask what it is at 45! Although these may seem impossible amounts, they are just about what is put into most final salary schemes. And remember, baby steps. Better to save something than nothing.

If you pay into an employer's pension scheme, you can pay extra contributions into a separate pension. If you can buy 'added years', do that. Otherwise the best thing to do is to pay into a stakeholder pension (see below), as the charges are capped. In the past these add-on pensions were called AVCs, which stands for additional voluntary contributions. But these tend to be more expensive and less flexible than stakeholder. For example, when you retire you can take a quarter of your stakeholder fund as a tax-free lump sum. With the old AVCs you could not normally do that. Until April 2006, you cannot put money into a stakeholder if you pay into a company pension scheme and earn more than £30,000 a year. But these restrictions will end in April 2006 and it is better to go for stakeholder if you can.

Personal and stakeholder pensions

Nowadays, anyone can pay into a pension whether they work or not. Personal pensions were introduced in 1988 and began with a scandal that has cost the industry £13 billion to put right. Millions of people were encouraged to leave their company schemes and put money into a personal pension instead, which, for most people, was bad advice and around two million people were paid £11 billion compensation (the other £2 billion was the cost of administering the compensation scheme). But that should not put you off investing in a pension now.

Nowadays, almost all personal pensions have the 'stakeholder' label, which means that the pension follows certain rules laid down by the government. The most important is that the charges are capped at 1 per cent a year. This cap will rise to 1.5 per cent a year after April 2005, though many will still operate at 1 per cent and you can still find schemes that charge less. You can think of charges as being like a leak in the bottom of a tank you are trying to fill. As you put water in at the top, there is a steady drip drip drip from the bottom. The bigger the drip, the longer it will take to fill the tank. The lower the charges, the less money will be drained away from your fund each year.

Every employer with more than four staff members that does not have a company scheme has to make arrangements for its staff to pay into a stakeholder pension. However, the employer does not have to pay into this scheme, and the stakeholder scheme they have set up may not have the best charges or terms. You are better off finding your own and paying into it direct.

Personal and stakeholder pensions work like money purchase schemes – except that your employer is not paying in as well. You pay money into the fund and it is invested for you. When you reach your fifties you can start drawing your pension, though it is much more sensible to wait until you are 70. From 2010, the lowest age to draw the pension will be raised to 55.

At the moment there are restrictions on how much you can put into a stakeholder scheme. These depend on your age, and rise from 17.5 per cent of your earnings up to age 35, to 40 per cent at 60 and over. From April 2006 these limits are being scrapped and you will be able to pay in virtually what you like. However, you cannot put in more than your annual pay and there is an overall upper limit of £215,000 a year. Not a worry for most of us!

If you are neither an employee nor a self-employed person, you can only pay in a maximum of £3600 a year into a stakeholder pension. Anyone can do this – and you can do it for someone else. So if you and your partner have children and one of you looks after them while the other works, then the one with the income can put money into a stakeholder pension for their partner. Similarly you can invest in a stakeholder pension for a child.

The way the money is paid into a stakeholder – or now a personal – pension is odd. You pay in, say, £100 a month. The Chancellor then boosts this with the tax you have already paid on that, adding another £28.20 (arithmetic alert! See below). If you are a higher-rate taxpayer – three million people are – the Chancellor adds another £66.67. That's not because better-paid people are more than twice as important to the Chancellor as those who earn less, it's because … actually, I can't think why. And when I have asked politicians or officials, they haven't been able to explain it either. Government figures show that out of the £14 billion a year that this tax relief costs, more than half of it goes to the richest 10 per cent of taxpayers. So there must be a reason. I just don't know what it is. Perhaps your MP can explain it to you.

Arithmetic alert Why does the Chancellor add £28.20 when the rate of tax is 22 per cent? Look at it this way. Your boss gives you an extra £100. Before you see a penny of it the Chancellor takes off, as you say, 22 per cent in tax. So you get paid an extra £100 but after tax you only take home £78.

When you put money into a pension, you don't have to pay tax on it. So if you pay £100 into your stakeholder pension, the Chancellor has to give you back the tax you have already paid. So how much do you have to earn to have £100 left after tax? Now we know it isn't £100 because you only have £78 left when you get an extra £100. So it's 100 x 100/78 = £128.20. You can see that's right by working out the tax due on £128.20 like this: 128.20 x 0.22 = £28.20. Deduct that and you have £100 left. So when you put £100 into your stakeholder, the Chancellor adds £28.20, which is the tax you have already paid on that money. And before you ask, no, he doesn't do the same with National Insurance contributions.

Stakeholders have not been the success the government hoped. But they have had a great effect on the old personal pensions, driving down charges for new customers to much the same sort of 1 per cent level. However, people who took out a personal pension before stakeholders began in April 2001 may be stuck with higher charges – which can easily be twice as much or more. So if you have a personal pension that dates from before April 2001, it is worth getting financial advice, checking the costs and moving your pension to a cheaper provider.

Keeping track

Nowadays people move jobs more often than ever. But whenever you move you can take your pension with you. If you have been paying into a final salary scheme for at least two years, you can get what is called a transfer value. That is the amount of money your pension is now worth, and you can move it to a new scheme. Or you can leave it where it is and claim the small pension when you retire. It's often hard to work out which is the best thing to do. A financial adviser – a good one – may be able to help.

If you have paid into a money purchase scheme you can also take that with you. After two years you will get the whole value including any contributions paid by your employer. The value of the fund has to be transferred into either another company scheme or into a personal pension. Some schemes will let you move the fund if you have been a member for less than two years. Others keep the contributions your employer has paid and return those you have paid – less tax.

If you lose touch with pensions you may have paid into in the past you can track them down through the Pension Schemes Registry, a government organization that has more than 200,000 schemes on its books. The more information you can give, the better the chance of tracking down your pension. They will need the name and address of any employer who might have run a scheme you belonged to. Information about that employer, such as whether it was part of a larger group or if it traded under any other names, will be helpful. Dates when you joined and left the scheme will also help.

Of course, the main question about any pension that you have paid into is: What pension will this buy me? And that, of course, is just the question that no one can answer. It depends on three things.

How big is your fund now? You can find this out from your fund-holder – and every April they should tell you.

When will you retire? This is up to you, but some schemes specify an age. Legally you can retire and draw your pension at any age between 50 and 75, though that changes to 55–75 from 2010. The longer you leave it the better – for your pension, if not your sanity. Every year you delay is one more year of paying in and nearly one less year of taking out (don't ask me why it is 'nearly' one less year of taking out, it just is).

How big will the fund be then? No one knows. But from April 2005 you will be given a clue – though not a very good one – in a pension statement that will be sent to you every year. This statement will show you how much is in your pension fund, how much might be in it if you retire at 65, and how big a pension that will buy you then. All these predictions depend on projections about the rate of growth of your investment. We will see later how meaningless these projections can be.

■ Financial advisers

Nowadays, everyone will come across a 'financial adviser'. I put the phrase in inverted commas because although some of the 148,000 registered advisers are extremely knowledgeable and will give you good advice in all circumstances, many others are not – and will not. Many cannot.

Despite their title, financial advisers are salespeople. Their job is to sell you stuff. And their advice is aimed to that end. You might as well call the bloke on a used-car lot a 'transportation consultant'. Or the spotty youth in a hi-fi shop an 'audiovisual counsellor'.

There are now three types of financial adviser:
- Independent
- Tied
- Multi-tied

Let's try that again:
- Free
- Shut in a room
- Allowed out on a lead

Let me explain. An **independent financial adviser** (IFA) has to be qualified and must give you advice about the most suitable financial product for your needs drawn from the whole range of every product on the UK market. A **tied agent** works for just one company and can only advise you about the products of that company – even if there are better products for you from another. So the Man from the Pru works just for Prudential, can only discuss Prudential products and that is all he can sell you.

So far so simple. But at the end of 2004 another category of financial salesperson was created: the **multi-tied** representative. A multi-tied representative sits somewhere in the middle between an IFA and a tied agent. And comes in two sorts. She might work for a High Street bank. But that bank might have an agreement to sell pensions from one insurance company, a savings product from another and a mortgage from a big building society. So although she works for one bank she can sell you a few other products from that bank's 'panel' of approved suppliers. Alternatively she might work for a financial advice agency. That agency will have done a deal with half a dozen big companies to sell pensions from one, investments from another, unit trusts from a third, endowments from number four, mortgages from number five and insurance from the last. Hence the name 'multi-tied' – though it is a title the industry hates, and one that will almost certainly never be used.

If you are with me so far, wait for a further stage in the changes to financial services that's happening in April 2005. All the sales staff mentioned so far have to be qualified – some are more qualified than others but they all have to have studied financial products and reached a certain level of expertise. But from April 2005 a new breed of unqualified salespeople will be let loose on an unsuspecting public. They can work for an independent, a tied or a multi-tied company. But they will be limited to selling you a small range of what are effectively government-approved, simple products usually called Sandler products, after the man, Ron Sandler, who invented them (see page 172), or perhaps 'stakeholder' products after … well, it is just a government word like 'modernization'.

They are supposed to be simple products with charges pegged below a certain level and with a lower risk than others, but this doesn't mean they are suitable for you. But if you are sold one that is not, it will be harder to get compensation.

You can see why these changes have been dubbed 'complification' by some industry wits. To summarize, from April 2005 there will be six types of person who can sell you financial products.

	Independent financial adviser	Multi-tied company	Single company
Qualified	Independent financial adviser	Qualified multi-tied representative	Qualified tied agent
Unqualified	Unqualified independent representative	Unqualified, multi-tied representative	Unqualified tied agent

It's important to know which of these six types of salesperson you are dealing with, but as you can see it gets a bit complicated. So the government has decided to simplify things. It has been decided that these six types will be called by just two different names:

	Independent financial adviser	Multi-tied company	Single company
Qualified	Independent financial adviser	Financial adviser	Financial adviser
Unqualified	Financial adviser	Financial adviser	Financial adviser

So someone who calls himself just a 'financial adviser' could be qualified or unqualified, could be genuinely independent, only able to sell you products from a panel of companies, or could be limited to the products of just one company. Only the phrase 'independent financial adviser' will mean a qualified and genuinely independent adviser.

Although the official names will not help, other new rules might. These make all financial advisers give you a document right at the start which sets out how they operate. Its formal name is an initial disclosure document, but it will probably be headed: 'Key facts about our services'. Here is how to decode it.

If it says the company deals with products from 'the whole market', it's an independent financial adviser. If it deals in products from a 'limited number' of companies, then it is a multi-tied representative, and somewhere it will tell you the names of the companies and the products of theirs it sells. Or it will say it can only sell you products from a single company – and it will tell you which one. The salesperson will also have to tell you if they are one of the unqualified breed who can only sell simple products. In which case, politely ask for someone else. Always.

The adviser will also give you what is called a menu card, setting out how the company is paid and what that will cost you. This menu should show the fees or the commission the company may receive. There should also be an indication of how those charges compare to the typical market rate. If there isn't one, ask.

My advice is always to stick with an independent financial adviser, or IFA. They do what it says on the label: they give you advice, about finance, that is independent. By law, no one else can do that. IFAs are legally obliged to find the most suitable product for their client after considering every single product on the market from every company in the UK. So if you need financial advice you should only ever go to an IFA. Everyone else will be partial and prevented by law from selling you a better product if it's produced by a company they do not have a link with. IFAs must now by law offer you the chance to pay them a fee for their time, as a cast-iron guarantee of their impartiality. Expect that to be £100 an hour. Be pleased if it's less, but don't be too surprised if it's more – especially in London.

Sadly, over the next few years, IFAs will become rarer and more exclusive, concentrating on what they like to call 'high net worth individuals'. In other words, rich folk. Happily, however, tied agents will decline in numbers too and will eventually all but disappear. The major banks and insurers who currently employ them will do deals with the big insurance companies and they will turn into multi-tied representatives. But they won't, of course, be called that.

And those men in the middle will flourish. The big insurance companies are desperate to get 'on the panel' of the major High Street banks and building societies. So the banks and building societies who have a retail presence on the High Street can cut a deal and get good terms from them. That means that you, the consumer, should get a good deal too. That's the theory. Certainly someone will make money.

■ Choosing an IFA

Once you have decided to see an IFA – after rejecting all those offers you might get from 'financial advisers' who are not independent – how do you go about it? Think of it like anything else. A pipe bursts. How do you choose a plumber? Yellow Pages? That bloke with a van you see round the corner sometimes? That card that was pushed through your door a while ago? The plumber who did your best friend's bathroom on time, at a reasonable cost and without making much mess?

Put like that it is a no-brainer, isn't it? Word-of-mouth recommendation from someone you know is the best way. Of course, not everyone has a handy friend who has already done the choosing – and risk-taking – for them. But even if you have, there is a big difference between plumbing and financial advice. Your friend might *think* she has got a good deal, but it will take a long time to find out whether she has, and she may turn out to be the victim of a plausible incompetent. Or a clever crook.

> I once visited a woman, in her seventies, who had been conned out of a lot of money by an IFA who visited her at home. I asked her about him. What was he like, did she have any suspicions about him? 'No,' she replied. 'He seemed such a nice man. He had a Rolls-Royce and every-thing.' She never wondered who had paid for it! He now lives abroad – and the woman I visited was lucky not to lose her home.

■ Checking for yourself

If someone tries to sell you financial products and you don't know them or where they are from, then you should *always* check up on them. In the past you could always check if an individual adviser was registered and approved or not. But now the unqualified people – in the bottom row of the table on page 187 – are not registered individually and you cannot find them on a list. However, the company they work for *must* be registered. And the qualified people in the top row must always be registered individually. You can check up on individuals or the firms they work for using the FSA website given in Follow-up, Investment, page 205. This also lists unauthorized firms and banks that are currently targeting UK investors (never use any of them) and has a helpful section on scams and swindles.

Better is to find someone yourself. The Follow-up section at the back of this book has several websites that will help. Once you have found your list of advisers, try to pick about five, call them and ask for an appointment at their office. The first interview is always free (if not, then don't even consider them). Never let the adviser come to your home. It is hard to get rid of people you have welcomed in and given tea and biscuits. If you don't like them it is much easier to leave their office than to ask them to leave your home. Also you can see how their operation works. Don't be too impressed with a smart office in an expensive location. Who's paying for it? Their clients, that's who.

> I went to see a large IFA company in its Mayfair office. Everything seemed very expensive, and the rent must have cost a small fortune. I was suspicious from the start, but particularly cautious when I was told the power had gone off so we had to do the interview in the lobby. The lights were on there. It turned out later that the company had not paid its bills and was soon in administration, taking with it millions of pounds of clients' money. Fortunately I was there as a journalist, not an investor.

Remember that all IFAs make their living by selling things to people like you. So they want you as a customer. If you don't buy much the first time there will be more business in the future. They will want to ask you lots of questions – partly to assess you and partly because it is a legal requirement. But you should also ask them questions.

What qualifications do they have? Do not be impressed by the Financial Planning Certificate (FPC) – that's the minimum requirement and every qualified adviser should have it or something similar. Better advisers have at least three units from the Advanced Financial Planning Certificate (AFPC), such as G60, which covers pensions, or G20 (personal financial planning). These are from the Chartered Insurance Institute, and there are other qualifications by other organizations, so don't be afraid to ask for a list and then check up on them using the internet.

Do they specialize in any particular areas, such as pensions, or low-risk investments, or mortgages?

What research does the firm use? Every IFA has to keep up with all new products and find the best. So more and more subscribe to commercial services that do that work for them.

You should also ask to speak to one or two of the firm's existing clients. If they will not let you – using the excuse of data protection or human rights or some such nonsense – then walk away.

Finally, see how you feel about them. Finance is a very personal business and it's essential that you like and trust the people you deal with.

Once you have picked an adviser and you get down to recommendations, you should be armed with another list of questions about what they are recommending.

- Why are you recommending this for me?
- What will I get out of the deal?
- Could I lose money and what are the chances I will?
- Are there any guarantees? If not, why not?
- What are the risks?
- What other recommendations did you consider and reject? Why?
- What will you (the adviser) get out of the deal?

Be aware all the time that financial advisers have sold people terrible things and often believed in them themselves. Here are some things to be cautious about:

Magic Never believe a promise of exceptional returns. If a deal seems too good to be true, it probably is.

Confusion Your adviser should be able to explain the details of your finances clearly and without jargon. If not, they probably don't understand them. And you should find an adviser who does.

Urgency Never be fooled by people who say you have to sign up immediately or risk losing a never-to-be-repeated deal. If you cannot take your time, just say no.

Churning This is the wonderful name for getting you to cash in existing investments to reinvest them in something similar. You will pay twice – in penalties for cancelling them and commission for starting something new. Most of the latter will go straight to your adviser for selling it to you. So that's why the IFAs do it.

Eggs in one basket Beware an IFA who wants to put a substantial part of your money in one place. It breaks the Golden and Sparkly Rule! Spread your investments. Recently the FSA suggested that no one should have more than a third of their investments in a single type of stock-market investment – and that was reduced to a fifth if it was their only stock-market investment.

Tax You should not invest in something just because it saves tax. Make sure it is right for you as an investment. Tax relief can always be taken away by a future government. And it will never make a bad investment good.

Payable to me Never make a cheque out to the adviser. Always make it out to the company you are investing in. If an adviser wants it made out to him or her or their company, walk away.

■ Lies, damn lies and projections

After your meeting your adviser will send you a letter setting out the reasons why the recommendations were made. Many people are surprised by this letter, which sometimes seems to bear no relation to the conversation they had. The letter will put in all the legal bits the adviser may not have mentioned, and if you subsequently want to make a complaint the letter will used as evidence that you agreed to the recommendations and were warned about the risks.

Do not sign it without reading it. Check especially the bit on your attitude to risk (see Two or three little words, page 164). Make sure your adviser has understood your feelings about losing money. Many people who have told their adviser they have a low to medium desire for risk have ended up with most of their money at risk in stock market-based investments.

The letter will make it clear that there is a cooling-off period when you can cancel the deal without penalty. If you are unhappy with the deal, cancel it now. Don't worry about hurting the IFA's feelings or about whether you have made a gentleman's agreement. If things do go wrong, the adviser or the company will only ever consider the legal position – not your feelings. You must do the same.

You will also be sent a document setting out the 'key features' of the product you have bought. This will explain its aims, risks and benefits, and set out the impact of charges and expenses. These documents are very long and can be confusing. Many people put them straight in a drawer and forget about them, which can be a mistake.

The document must also give numbers which 'illustrate' the projected growth of any investment and the impact of costs and charges. This section is always misleading because the estimated rates by which your money will 'grow' in the future are not promises – nor, indeed, even what the company that sold it to you believes. They are based on 'standard' rates of growth provided by the FSA, and these rates, which have not changed since 1999, are: 5 per cent, 7 per cent and 9 per cent for tax-free investments such as pensions and ISAs; and 4 per cent, 6 per cent and 8 per cent for all other investments that are normally taxed. Often you will see all three growth rates – shown perhaps as low, medium and high. There is absolutely no reason to believe that any of these rates will be achieved. They may be achieved, or not. They may be exceeded or never reached. There is no reason to believe that the middle rate will be achieved any more than that the low or the high one will. They are, in other words, meaningless. So do not count on them coming true.

Even if they did, consider this. The middle projection for tax-free savings is 7 per cent. From that the industry takes its charges, which can now be 1.5 per cent. That leaves 5.5 per cent per year as the central growth projection after charges. But you can earn 5.5 per cent in charge-free cash savings products, so why risk your money? Even if this projection is achieved, you will be no better off. Your adviser will have taken all the extra that has been earned. And you will have taken all the risk!

The good news is that the FSA has decided to review these misleading projection rates. Even though it stands by the middle rate for use at the time of writing, it admits that the higher and lower ones 'have no rational basis'. It's not clear at the moment how they will be changed. But whatever is decided, the changes will not happen for a while.

■ Scandals

> My financial adviser looked after my money as if it was his own. And
> pretty soon it was. *Anon*

Don't feel embarrassed about asking questions or being sceptical about what
you are told. Most financial advisers are honest individuals and genuinely
want to help you buy the right product. It's just that collectively their advice
has cost millions of people billions of pounds. No lawful industry has been
rocked by such a succession of scandals as financial services. Just look at the
big ones.

- ■ Mortgage endowments sold from the 1980s right up to the late
  1990s will leave three million people up to £50 billion short of the
  money they need to repay their mortgage. Only £1 billion of compensation has been paid.
- ■ Personal pensions mis-sold to nearly two million people from 1988 to
  1994 cost the industry £11.5 billion in compensation and another £2
  billion in running the compensation scheme.
- ■ Additional voluntary contributions – between 1988 and 1994 at least
  100,000 customers were sold the wrong sort of AVCs to top up their
  company pensions. More than £250 million in compensation has
  been paid.
- ■ Equitable Life – 400,000 policy holders with Equitable Life have faced
  a shortfall of £3 billion in what they expected.
- ■ Split capital investment trusts were sold as safe investments mainly
  from 1998 to 2002. Up to 50,000 individuals have lost at least £600
  million. Compensation of £350 million is being sought by the regulator.
- ■ Precipice bonds were sold between 1997 and 2004 to 450,000
  mainly older customers who wanted safety and a good return. They
  put in £7.4 billion and may have lost more than £2 billion.
- ■ With-profits policies – millions of investors in these policies have £80
  billion in closed funds with limited long-term growth prospects.

Apart from these seven major scandals over 20 years, in the last three years the FSA has fined 35 companies and individuals a total of £22.6 million and forced them to pay £327 million in compensation for a variety of activities ranging from the misleading to the illegal.

These are the old scandals. Don't be part of a future one. Make sure you read this before you go to see a financial adviser – independent, tied or multi-tied, qualified or not.

This is the beginning of the new financial you.

Paul Lewis

Chapter 8
Your financial action plan

❑ Goals

❑ Life plans

❑ Debt

❑ Saving and investing

Everything you have read in this book can be turned into a financial action plan that will keep you in control of your money – rather than the other way around – throughout your life. The first goal is to set goals. Sensible goals, goals that you can reach. Goals that you can walk towards with baby steps. One step at a time. One goal at a time. And remember, any saving is worthwhile. Know what you spend. Write it down. Then cut it down. One item at a time, one saving at a time. You will be surprised how it mounts up.

> John D. Rockefeller was at the time the richest man in the world. As he was leaving his hotel he saw a penny on the floor and bent down to pick it up. 'But, sir,' asked a reporter, 'why are you picking up that penny? It can mean nothing to you.' Rockefeller looked at him. 'Young man, if I hadn't, I would be a penny poorer for the rest of my life, wouldn't I?'

■ Life

Save for your children. And teach them about money. Passing on knowledge is what makes humans progress. If you have babies, claim what money you can. It's there for the taking. Buying a home has never been a bad idea financially, but don't try to time it for financial reasons. Buy it when you need it. You may have to stretch but make sure you can afford it.

When you are in a relationship, keep your eyes open. Marry or not. But be aware of the legal and financial differences and make sure you are happy with them. If the relationship ends, be fair about money. You'll be happier in the long run. Whatever else you hide or don't talk about, never ignore money. That could end the best thing that ever happened to you.

■ Debt

Ultimately get rid of it. But that's a big goal, a hard one that takes giant steps. So look for the baby steps. First, understand it. Learn the difference between good debt and bad debt. Learn how to use debt. Find the cheap debt. And avoid the debt traps set by the banks to snare the unwary. Never turn good debt in to bad debt by securing it on your home. And remember – borrowing to pay off a loan is not paying off a loan!

Second, never ignore it. Talk to the banks. Talk to your partner. Talk first to yourself.

Third, master it. Rank your debts. Then get rid of them, one at a time.

■ Saving

Or is it investing? Learn the difference. Saved money remains yours. Invested money is someone else's. Never forget that. You can earn money on your savings, safely. They will build up. The kind of savings plan depends not on what you want but when you want it. Save for the time, not the purpose. Only long-term savings are worth taking a risk with.

Learn about risk. It means you can lose your money, certainly some of it, possibly all of it. It also may mean you can make a better return than you can with cash. That is the nature of risk. Some you win, some you lose.

If you want to invest, hitch your savings wagon to the whole stock market. If anything is going to go steadily up over the long term, it is that. And the leak in your piggy bank – known as charges and commission – will be less. Find an adviser who is qualified and whom you trust. If it sounds too good to be true, it almost certainly is. And remember the scandals. Don't be part of a future one.

I WOULD WRITE 'THE END'.
I BELIEVE IT IS TRADITIONAL AT THIS POINT.
BUT THIS IS NOT THE END.
IT IS THE BEGINNING.
OF THE NEW FINANCIAL YOU.
GOOD LUCK WITH IT.

Follow-up

Everything in this book can be followed up by looking at websites, calling helplines, reading further, or listening to radio and TV programmes.

Lots of the stuff can be followed up by doing a search on the web using Google. Google searches more than 4 billion web pages. If you do not know it, then log on to www.google.com and try it out. Put in 'state pension forecast' and see what it brings up. If you use www.google.co.uk you can confine it to UK websites only. Once you have decided it is the best invention since the electric guitar, download the Google toolbar and have it available on your web browser all the time. *Hint*: if you want to find an exact phrase put it in quotes thus: 'Paul Lewis'. There are some mad people with the same name as me. See if you can guess which one I am.

Here are the websites and phone numbers you may not find so easily with Google – though some of them you will.

Bank accounts

You can find out which banks pay the best rates on current accounts – and which charge the least for overdrafts – at www.moneyfacts.co.uk and www.moneysupermarket.com. You can also compare at the website run by the Consumers Association: www.switchwithwhich.co.uk. These are the best sites for comparing current accounts. But remember, commercial internet Best Buy tables make money when you click on a link to another site. Remember, too, that they don't include the whole market. Some financial organizations are missed out by mistake. Others have asked to be omitted. And occasionally, just sometimes, they are left out for commercial reasons – either because they won't pay to be there or there is some dispute going on. So try two or three comparison sites and never just go for the top one without checking out exactly what you are getting and why it is top.

The banks all subscribe to a Code of Practice about how they should treat us all, including how easy it should be to change banks. You can read the code and if you have problems with a bank, you can either complain here: www.bankingcode.org.uk, or you can call on 020 7661 9694.

Switching electricity or gas

Energywatch is the consumer body for gas and electricity users. Log on at www.energywatch.org.uk or call 08459 06 07 08. You can get lists of the tariffs in your area as well as help with disputes with energy suppliers.

Ofgem is the government regulator for gas and electricity: log on to www.ofgem.gov.uk or call 0845 906 0708.

If you want to switch your gas or electricity supplier to a cheaper tariff there are nine approved websites that help you make the switch. You can get a list on the Energywatch website >help and advice >saving money >click here. Or just try one of them. Log on to www.uswitch.com or call 0800 093 0607.

Water

Water UK represents the industry and is at www.water.org.uk or call 020 7344 1844. There are links there to local water companies; or do a Google search. There is also a consumer body WaterVoice which you find through the water regulator www.ofwat.gov.uk

Phones

If you have your phone bills to hand, and know who you call and when, log on to www.uswitch.co.uk and get an estimate of the cheapest way to make your calls.

www.switchwithwhich.co.uk does the same for mobile phones. Perhaps they employ Stephen Hawking!

TV

If you are a masochist, spend a couple of hours on www.sky.co.uk trying to find the cheapest way to get Sky. You can find out more about the free digital TV service from www.freeview.co.uk or you can call 08708 80 99 80. Or find out about cable in your area from www.telewest.co.uk 0800 953 5383 or www.ntl.com 0800 183 0123. Don't pay for channels you don't watch!

Insurance

If you really want insurance, make sure you get the cheapest. A good place to start is www.insuresupermarket.com.

The Inland Revenue

If you want to claim tax back from your savings call the Inland Revenue helpline 0845 980 0645. Or you can find it on the Inland Revenue website: www.inlandrevenue.gov.uk/taxback. In fact, the Inland Revenue website is full of useful stuff – giving you online access to leaflets and forms and infor-mation. Log on to www.inlandrevenue.gov.uk or find your local Inland Revenue Enquiry Centre in your phone book. Alternatively, you can check out the list of tax helplines at www.inlandrevenue.gov.uk/menus/helpline.htm.

The Land Registry

You can contact the Land Registry at 020 7917 8888 or www.landreg.gov.uk to find out all sorts of things – including what your neighbours paid for their house – but particularly to check details of your house ownership.

Buying a home

Compare mortgages at the familiar www.moneyfacts.co.uk and also www.moneysupermarket.com and www.fsa.gov.uk/tables. Check out Stamp Duty Land Tax at www.inlandrevenue.gov.uk/so.

Council tax

Your local council is the place to go and the helpline number will be on the council tax bill you were sent. You can also check up what help you might get with your tax at the can't-praise-it-enough website www.entitledto.co.uk.

Students

The Student Loans Company has a useful website: www.slc.co.uk. The government site for England and Wales is www.dfes.gov.uk/studentsupport. In Scotland check out www.student-support-saas.gov.uk. For an alternative view, try www.nusonline.co.uk and www.support4learning.org.uk/money.

Reaching 50

Can I mention an excellent guide here called *The Complete Money Plan* from Age Concern aimed at those heading for retirement, probably quicker than they want to!

You can download a free 32-page version at www.ageconcern.org.uk or buy the whole thing for £6.99. I think it is excellent because (a) I wrote it and (b) it is! I get no royalties. So buying it just helps Age Concern.

Child benefit and tax credit

You can find out more about what you can get at the Inland Revenue website www.inlandrevenue.gov.uk, or try the much more user-friendly site www.entitledto.co.uk. Or you can ring the Inland Revenue tax credit helpline on 0845 300 3900, or 0845 603 2000 in Northern Ireland.

Other benefits

You can try the government website at www.dwp.gov.uk, although it's not as user-friendly as it might be. You can find out about disability benefits from the Disability Alliance www.disabilityalliance.org or call 020 7247 8763, though it is only open a few hours a week. For education maintenance allowances, call the EMA helpline 080 810 16 2 19. And you can find out more about other financial help for 16- to 19-year-olds still at school or college on www.dfes.gov.uk/financialhelp.

Couples

A useful website called www.advicenow.co.uk has a whole section on living together. And how to protect yourself if you are not married. If worst comes to worst, married or not, you can find lawyers who will help end relationships fairly and peacefully through the Solicitors Family Law Association at www.sfla.org.uk, or by calling 01689 850227.

And of course www.relate.org.uk can offer help as well. There will be a local branch in your phone book too.

Redundancy

Lots of places to go for help.

Official stuff: www.dti.gov.uk/er/redundancy.htm.

Redundancy Payments helpline: 0845 145 00 04.

Advice: ww.adviceguide.org.uk/index/life/employment/redundancy.htm.

Employer goes bust: www.insolvency.gov.uk.

Commercial site: www.redundancyhelp.co.uk.

Credit reference agencies

You can get a copy of the credit information stored by the three credit reference agencies for £2, though they will try to sell you more expensive versions and even get you to subscribe for regular credit checks.

Equifax plc: log on to www.equifax.co.uk or call 0845 600 1772.

Experian ltd: log on to www.uk.experian.com or call 0870 2416212.

Callcredit plc: log on to www.callcredit.plc.uk or call 0870 060 1414.

Credit cards

The very best credit card site for information and advice is this one: www.moneysavingexpert.com. It gets a bit overexcited at times but the advice is sound and up-to-date and you can sign up for a regular email with money-saving tips on a variety of subjects.

For simply finding the best buys on credit cards or on loans use www.moneyfacts.co.uk, though it sometimes misses out information and does not include all cards. An alternative is www.moneysupermarket.com, which also misses out some best buys. But it does offer special deals on which it earns commission.

Debt

If you get into debt difficulties, the three free national organizations you should consider are: Consumer Credit Counselling Service (www.cccs.co.uk

or call 0800 138 1111); National Debtline (www.nationaldebtline.co.uk or 0808 808 4000), or your local branch of the Citizen's Advice Bureau (find this at www.nacab.org.uk or in the phone book).

Mortgage brokers

There are loads of local and national mortgage brokers. Check your broker is registered with the Financial Services Authority at www.fsa.gov.uk/consumer/fcs/index.html. Here are two that I think are good. Both have calculators showing how much you can borrow and offer advice and information.

www.charcolonline.co.uk guides you through finding the right mortgage and has special offers that can be very good value. If you do it all through the website there is no fee to arrange a mortgage. But if you talk to an advisor at Charcol, then there is a fee. Their number is 0800 71 81 91.

London & Country – or L&C as it prefers to be called now – is a national broker that does not charge you a fee. The website www.lcplc.co.uk is very good or you can speak to a person on 0800 953 0304.

Saving – for you or for the kids

You can find the best buy savings accounts at www.moneyfacts.co.uk and www.moneysupermarket.com. There is also an 'official' site I really like at www.fsa.gov.uk/tables. Ask it to sort the deals by interest rate, not alphabetically.

You can find out about all the National Savings and Investments products on its website www.nsandi.com or by calling 0845 964 5000.

Investments

For government stock (gilts) go to www.dmo.gov.uk, or call the Bank of England on 0800 818 614 to get an application form.

For ethical investments, contact the Social Investment Forum www.uksif.org or the Ethical Investment Research Service at www.eiris.org. You can get good advice and interesting information from Motley Fool at www.fool.co.uk – but it is a bit overwhelmed by adverts and click-through offers.

You can check up on the credentials of financial advisers and the firms they work for using the list at www.fsa.gov.uk/consumer/fcs/index.html or by calling 0845 606 1234.

To find an Independent Financial Adviser (IFA), there are five websites you can use but they vary in quality and usefulness.

www.unbiased.co.uk will find you the nearest IFAs from the 10,500 on the books of IFA Promotions. You can choose how you want to pay your IFA and pick some of the qualifications they may have. Put in your postcode and get the six that fit the criteria nearest to you. You can also ring IFA Promotions on 0800 085 3250.

www.sofa.org (not www.sofa.org.uk which is, well, sofas!) is run by the Society of Financial Advisers, SOFA, which considers its members a cut above others. Put in your postcode and find the nearest members.

www.financialplanning.org.uk The Institute of Financial Planning organizes training and qualifications – the Certificate in Financial Planning – for IFAs. So its members consider themselves better than run of the mill IFAs. But the website only asks for the region you live in, and provides a list of dozens of planners which makes it hard to choose three to try out.

www.searchifa.co.uk is a commercial site – 14,000 IFAs pay to be on it – and it offers seven IFAs near to your postcode. But it only asks for the first letters of your code so the companies offered could be miles away. It is not clear how the seven are chosen. It is the only site where you can search specifically for a female IFA.

www.fba.co.uk is from a new organization called Fee Based Advice, whose members are all IFAs who only charge fees rather than commission. They tend to deal with wealthier clients. You can find the nearest in your region through its website.

Pensions

To find out what your state pension will be contact the State Pension Forecasting Service (0845 3000 168 or find it at www.thepensionservice.gov.uk).

If you've lost track of a pension from a past employer, call 0191 225 6316 (ask for a tracing request form) or log on to www.opra.gov.uk/traceAPension.

For pension questions or problems, try the Pensions Advisory Service (OPAS): www.opas.org.uk.

Print and broadcast

Most newspapers now have a personal finance section on Saturday, Sunday and often on Wednesday too. The *Guardian* 'Jobs and Money' (Saturday), the *Daily Telegraph* 'Your Money' (Saturday), and the *Daily Mail* 'Money Mail' (Wednesday) are among the best.

Money Box, which I present on Radio 4 (Saturdays 12 noon), is an award-winning personal finance programme with news and advice about making the most of your money. *Money Box Live* is our phone-in (Mondays 3pm). Both can be heard at any time at www.bbc.co.uk/moneybox. Also very good is *Working Lunch* on BBC2 weekdays at lunchtime, with financial news and information.

More essential guides available in the Personal Development series from BBC Books:

Be Creative: Essential Steps to
Revitalize
Your Work and Life
Guy Claxton and Bill Lucas
Publication date: March 2004
ISBN: 0563 48764 X
CD ISBN: 0563 52331 X

Get Up and Do It!: Essential Steps
to Achieving Your Goals
Beechy and Josephine Colclough
Publication date: March 2004
ISBN: 0563 48765 8
CD ISBN: 0563 52346 8

The Confidence Plan: Essential Steps
to A New You
Sarah Litvinoff
Publication date: March 2004
ISBN: 0563 48763 1
CD ISBN: 0563 52336 0

Find the Balance: Essential Steps
to Fulfilment in Your Work and Life
Deborah Tom
Publication date: March 2004
ISBN: 0563 52138 4
CD ISBN: 0563 52341 7

Starting Out: Essential Steps
to Your Dream Career
Philippa Lamb and Nigel Cassidy
Publication date: August 2004
ISBN: 0563 52140 6
CD ISBN: 0563 52389 1

Agree to Win: Essential Steps
to Negotiate in Your Work and Life
Hugh Willbourn
Publication date: August 2004
ISBN: 0563 52148 1

Embracing Change: Essential Steps
to Make Your Future Today
Tony Buzan
Publication date: January 2005
ISBN: 0563 48762 3

All titles are available at good bookstores and online through the BBC shop at www.bbcshop.com